IMAGES of America
STEINWAY & SONS

On the Cover: "Grand bellymen" work on Steinway grand pianos at the New York factory in 1908. (Courtesy La Guardia and Wagner Archives.)

IMAGES of America
STEINWAY & SONS

Laura Lee Smith
Foreword by Michael Feinstein

Copyright © 2020 by Laura Lee Smith
ISBN 978-1-4671-0486-9

Published by Arcadia Publishing
Charleston, South Carolina

Library of Congress Control Number: 2019955540

For all general information, please contact Arcadia Publishing:
Telephone 843-853-2070
Fax 843-853-0044
E-mail sales@arcadiapublishing.com
For customer service and orders:
Toll-Free 1-888-313-2665

Visit us on the Internet at www.arcadiapublishing.com

For the men and women who build Steinway pianos and for the artists who play them—you bring beauty to the world.

Contents

Foreword		6
Acknowledgments		7
Introduction		8
1.	From Germany to America: Steinway Arrives in New York City	9
2.	Henry E. Steinway's Vision: To Build the Best Piano Possible	21
3.	Wealth, Power, and Prestige: A Legacy Takes Shape	39
4.	Craft and Creativity: The Rise of the Steinway Artisan	53
5.	Steinway Village: The Company Comes to Astoria	65
6.	Steinway Hall: Center of Music and Culture	81
7.	A Time of Transition: Steinway during the War	99
8.	People and Pianos: Steinway through the Decades	113

Foreword

There are names, and there are *names*.

Steinway definitely falls into the latter category. Most everyone knows that it denotes the highest art of piano manufacturing and has been ever thus practically since Genesis. Steinway's time-honored logo is borne from generations of hard work, and its gold-lettered font offers instant comfort to anyone who sits before it at the keyboard.

When I was in my late teens back in my hometown of Columbus, Ohio, I participated in a community theater show about the Marx Brothers that culminated with me at the keyboard center stage, portraying the piano-playing Marx brother, Chico. One night, the cast changed the ornate logo on the music box, substituting the gilt-lettered Steinway logo and trademarked lyre for another carefully stenciled script that read "Feinsteinway," and underneath in smaller letters was "schmuck," a Yiddish word not for the faint of heart. My reaction to it caused a ripple among the entire cast that proved the Shakespearean phrase "what's in a name" to be true.

If you live in New York, you are aware of Steinway Place, which is still home to the majestic old Steinway factory, methodically producing pianos in its time-honored old-fashioned way with master craftsmen who deftly combine classic and contemporary sensibilities in their work.

Just across the way from the large factory complex sits the once-grand former Steinway family mansion, crying out from the past for salvation. One can imagine what life was once like there, and viewing it leaves you with a deep yearning to know the story of the glamorous ghosts one can feel inhabiting the space.

This lovely book reveals the extraordinary Steinway history, filled with classic pictures accompanying a story of determination, hope, dreams, and love. It is as much about the American dream as it is about belief in possibilities and sharing the excitement of creating something that will bring change to the world and make it a fundamentally better place for all.

What a time that was!

As long as Steinway continues to make pianos, that dream can never be lost.

—Michael Feinstein
November 12, 2019

Acknowledgments

In 2008, I received a call from a former client, an entrepreneur for whom I'd written copy some years prior. When he told me he was working with Steinway & Sons and needed a copywriter to help in marketing, I sat up straight. "*The* Steinway & Sons?" I asked. "The *only* Steinway & Sons," he said. That was Todd Sanders on the phone, who is now Steinway's vice president of sales and marketing and is the man who brought me, a dozen years ago, into the fast-paced world of marketing the world's most revered musical instrument. To Todd, first and foremost, I owe sincere thanks, for without his faith in my abilities and his continued partnership, I would not have the privilege of spending my days writing about Steinway or the opportunity to have authored this book. I am also grateful beyond measure to Anthony Gilroy, Steinway's senior director of marketing, for his day-to-day leadership, poise, and good humor as we work together on all things Steinway, including the research and production of this history. Thanks are due to the many brilliant colleagues who have informed my knowledge of Steinway & Sons through the years, including but not limited to Elizabeth Olson, Leana Paymar, Dan Miceli, Ben Finane, Jackie Fugere, Vivian Chiu, Jim Hoover, Glen Gough, and Bob Rinaldi. Oversized thanks are due to David Kirkland for applying his deep knowledge of Steinway history to a careful review of this manuscript. A thank you is owed to Douglas DiCarlo and the archivists at the La Guardia and Wagner Archives, which holds a vast collection of Steinway photographs and documents. Unless otherwise noted, all images appear courtesy of La Guardia and Wagner Archives. Thanks and respect go to Dr. Richard Lieberman for his consummate history, *Steinway & Sons*, which was my guiding light. Finally, thanks are due to my family for their unwavering support: my mother, Judy Cook (proofreader extraordinaire); my children, Gemma and Iain Smith and Abi Coghill; and my husband, Chris Smith, who served with me in Steinway marketing for more than a decade and who, God love him, can even play a little piano.

INTRODUCTION

The legacy of the world's greatest piano-maker began more than two centuries ago in a tiny hamlet in north Germany, where Heinrich Engelhard Steinweg—later Henry E. Steinway—was born in 1797. His was a remarkable life story, one filled with early family tragedy, stiff odds of success, and a resiliency that allowed young Steinway to not only survive but to thrive as a cabinetmaker and organ-builder before trying his hand at piano construction. Steady but constrained local success for two decades eventually had Steinway and his piano-building sons looking toward the horizon for greater prospects. Germany's guild system and political unrest were frustratingly limiting for the ambitious Henry Steinway, and there soon seemed one clear solution: America.

When the Steinways arrived in New York City in the spring of 1850, they were part of a wave of more than 80,000 Germans to immigrate to America that year, and these Germans brought with them a passion for classical music that had yet to be developed in the United States. The new thirst for musical culture coincided with the rise of a middle class and unprecedented leisure time that allowed droves of Americans to purchase pianos. It was a perfect storm; the Steinways were in the right place at the right time.

However, it is interesting to note that the Steinway family did not start their own business immediately after landing in America. For three years, Henry and his sons Charles, Henry, William, and Albert worked for other piano manufacturers in New York with an eye toward learning the latest American techniques and acclimating to their new surroundings. The strategy proved wise. When the Steinways set up their own shop in a rented building on Varick Street in 1853, they were impatient with selling their skills to others, comfortable with American culture, and energized to compete. They were also imbued with a perfectionism that drove them into relentless pursuit of better piano design. The result was a completely new instrument, featuring technical advances never before seen in piano manufacturing. Indeed, Steinway & Sons did more than develop a historic brand—they literally developed the modern piano, and their patents and techniques are still in use to this day.

What makes Steinway & Sons such a uniquely American success story is the company's nimble-minded, no-holds-barred approach to both advancing the quality of its product and utterly dominating the marketplace. In addition to revolutionizing the modern piano, Steinway & Sons—and son William, in particular—revolutionized piano marketing, adopting a strategy of concert development and artist endorsements that persists to this day and that successfully positions Steinway as the piano of choice for the world's most revered professional pianists, both living and immortal.

William's business acumen and his brothers' technical prowess were a powerful combination. By the late 19th century, Steinway was a household name, and the family had settled into tremendous wealth and high visibility as the heads of a newly minted piano empire. Of course, the next century was not without challenges. Recessions, strikes, wars, family feuds, illness, and competition would plague the company through the decades, but in a testament to its remarkable tenacity, Steinway & Sons weathered every storm.

Today, in the world of musical instruments, there are pianos—and there is *Steinway*. Every piano that leaves the New York factory is a hand-crafted work of art that has taken nearly a year to produce, and Steinway is the overwhelming choice of professional concertizing pianists. As Michael Feinstein notes in his foreword, the name "Steinway" has veritably eclipsed itself—catapulting into that rare category of words that signify far more than their original meanings. Steinway is a family name, to be sure. But Steinway is also a piano, a place, an artistic grail, a status symbol, and a legend. The pages that follow explain why.

One

From Germany to America
Steinway Arrives in New York City

In the mid-19th century, America fell permanently in love with the piano. Though the instrument was invented in Italy some 150 years earlier, throughout the 1700s and early 1800s, pianos were the property of only the very wealthy, both in Europe and in the growing cities of the United States. But the Industrial Revolution and the rise of a middle class created a robust market for the piano not only as a source of music but also as a symbol of social standing and newly discovered leisure. It was toward this enthusiastic clamor for pianos that the Steinway family deliberately charted its course in 1850, leaving its provincial hometown in Germany for the financial attractions of New York City. Patriarch Heinrich Engelhard Steinweg, as he was known then, was no up-and-comer. He was a financially established cabinetmaker and piano-builder in central Germany and a middle-aged father of nine. But he was also a driven businessman who could see clearly that the political and economic climate of his home country could never offer the same promise of fortune as the market on the other side of the Atlantic. In 1850, accompanied by most of his family, he set sail for America. Three years later, when Steinway & Sons opened its doors, the most famous name in the history of piano manufacturing and marketing was born.

A survivor of Napoleon's occupation of Germany, Heinrich Engelhard Steinweg was born in 1797 in the north German hamlet of Wolfshagen. His mother and young siblings died of exposure while the family was in hiding from the French army in the freezing Harz Mountains, and his father (a forester) and brother were later killed in a fire. By age 15, orphaned and without prospects, Heinrich joined the army. Two years later, he participated in the Battle of Waterloo, where legend claims he was the bugler to announce the charge on Napoleon's troops in the battle that ended the Napoleonic Wars, earning a bronze medal for "Bugling in the Face of the Enemy." Following his military service, Heinrich learned woodworking and served an apprenticeship for a church organ–builder, where his interest in piano-building was sparked through an acquaintance with the church cantor's son. He established an organ business in 1829 and was soon prospering. This portrait was taken in Manhattan in 1850, after Heinrich and his family arrived in America. The Steinwegs would soon Americanize their name to "Steinway."

In the mid-1830s, Heinrich Steinweg started his first piano company in Seesen, Germany, and he did well, producing as many as 10 instruments per year and attaching this maker's label to every piano. However, the restrictiveness of the guild system in Seesen, combined with the crippled economy of post-revolution Germany, soon inspired Heinrich to consider America as a more promising location for his business.

This piano, often called the "Seesen Piano," or "Kitchen Piano," is one of the earliest known pianos built by cabinetmaker Heinrich Steinweg. Constructed in 1836 in the kitchen of Steinweg's home in Seesen, the piano was at one time on display at the New York Metropolitan Museum of Art and as of this writing is housed in the Musical Instrument Museum in Scottsdale, Arizona.

Heinrich married Julianne Thiemer in 1825. It was reported that Heinrich played the organ for his own wedding and that he gifted his bride with a hand-built square piano. The Steinwegs would raise 10 children in a handsome three-story home in Seesen, though one daughter died in infancy. In New York, Julianne was instrumental as an assistant to her husband, who spoke only German, in the early years of the business.

By the late 1840s, Steinweg's future in his economically depressed home country was unpromising. On July 1, 1850, Heinrich and Julianne, along with five of their children, arrived in New York on the maiden voyage of the steamship *Helena Sloman*. Oldest son C.F. Theodore stayed behind in Germany. A few months later, on its third voyage between Hamburg and New York, the ship sank, and nine people drowned.

Christian Friedrich Theodor Steinweg, later known as C.F. Theodore Steinway, was the Steinwegs' eldest child, born in Seesen in 1825. With his brother Henry Jr., Theodore attended Seesen's finest school and, by age 14, was developing a valuable talent as a pianist that his father put to use as they demonstrated their early pianos at exhibitions. This photograph was likely taken in Germany in the 1870s.

Second son Charles G. was the first of the family to come to America, having been sent to New York in 1849 to investigate opportunities for his piano-making family. He worked as a piano technician and wrote home regularly, reporting on business opportunities but omitting the harshest news: a cholera epidemic, violent unrest from working-class Irish, and horrific sanitation. He served in the New York State Militia during the Civil War.

The third son of Heinrich and Julianne, Henry Jr., was a brilliant piano engineer. The developments in his innovative "Steinway system"—most notably a patented overstrung grand piano, a cast-iron plate with agraffes, and a double-escapement action—changed piano manufacturing forever. In 1865, Henry died of tuberculosis at the age of 34. His widow, Ernestine, would soon enter a contentious custody battle for her three daughters with Henry's younger brother William.

Two years before his death, Henry Jr. became an American citizen. He was renowned as one of the greatest piano-builders of his time. "Mr. Steinway had reduced the manufacture of piano-forte to a science," wrote the *New York Times* in Henry's obituary, "and it is possible that few men ever lived who were better acquainted with the construction of the instrument." This document is dated January 28, 1863.

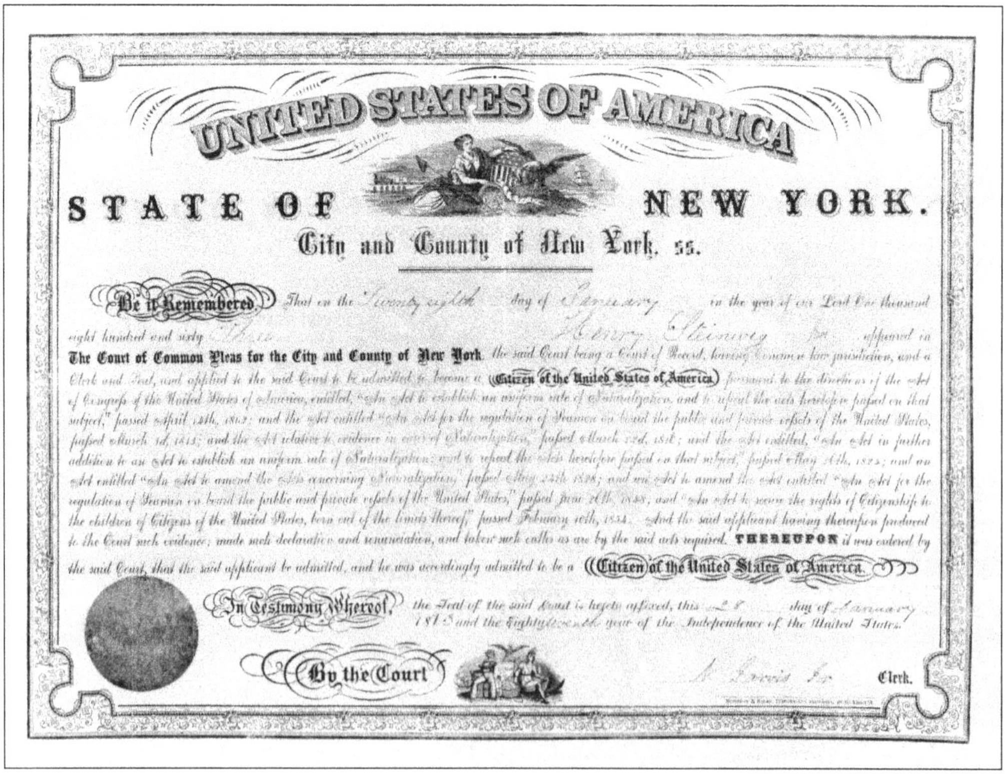

William Steinway (1835–1896) became one of the most Americanized members of the Steinway family. He spoke English easily and embraced the business and social cultures of New York City, often socializing with other successful German immigrants, including toy retailer F.A.O. Schwarz. His acumen in marketing, business operations, and communication contributed enormously to the growth of Steinway & Sons, and he directed the company from 1871 until 1896.

Though he was a gifted administrator and technical innovator, the achievements of Albert Steinway (1840–1877) were often overshadowed by those of his older brothers. Patriarch Henry E. Steinway and brothers Charles G. and Henry Jr. had already passed when Albert died of typhoid fever in 1877, leaving William and Theodore to run the family business.

Doretta Steinway Ziegler (1827–1900), Henry E. Steinway's oldest daughter, was an early salesperson for Steinway & Sons. She is mentioned frequently in her brother William's diary as a strong pillar of the Steinway family. A skilled pianist and teacher, she is honored today through Steinway & Sons' "Doretta Steinway University" experience for piano teachers.

Wilhelmina Steinway (1833–1875) was the second daughter of Henry and Julianne. Like most women of her time, the men in her family defined her life. Her first husband was Theodore Clemens Friedrich Vogel, a Steinway factory superintendent. After his death, she married opera singer William Candidus; they had three children together.

The entire staff of Steinway & Sons posed for this portrait in front of the factory at 82 Walker Street in 1858. Henry E. Steinway's former employer Pirsson previously had a piano factory at this site, so it was already equipped for piano manufacturing when the Steinways took it over. Sons Charles and William had also worked for another piano manufacturer, Nunns, at the same location. This building is in the middle of what is now Chinatown, but the street was then known as New York's "Piano Row." At this site, the Steinways began to develop their most important manufacturing processes. Most of the pianos built at this site were squares. The Steinways did not manufacture their first grand piano until 1856.

The family had been in New York for eight years when William purchased a large site on East Fifty-Third Street in 1858 to build a larger Steinway piano factory, which opened two years later. This purchase followed several years in which the family had rented space to build pianos, but costs for industrial rentals were rising, and it made fiscal sense to purchase land. By this time, Steinway & Sons was prospering, with a net worth of $75,000. The Steinways also built a row of brownstone homes on the same site. Here, the family poses in front of their homes next to the Steinway factory (background). Henry and Julianne; Henry Jr. and his wife, Ernestine; and William and his wife, Regina, stand on the steps of their homes. Charles G. and his wife, Sophie, are in the carriage. This photograph was taken in 1862. Today, the Seagram Building sits on the site of this factory.

The historic role of women in the Steinway family provides a fascinating window into societal mores of the 19th century. While Steinway women were consistently recorded as energetic contributors to the family business, their position in terms of power was modest, at best. Pictured at right is Regina Roos Steinway, William Steinway's first wife. The Steinways were so concerned about keeping control of the company within the family (especially as they watched Charles and other family members depart for service in the Civil War) that they required all Steinway wives to sign an agreement waiving their right to inherit shares in the company in the event of the death of their husbands, thus precluding potential transfer of ownership through any subsequent marriages. While the agreement granted the wives monetary compensation and employment, if desired, they were denied any share of the business. The 1863 agreement excerpted below spells out the terms. It was signed by Henry Jr. and his wife, Ernestine; Charles and his wife, Sophia; and William and Regina.

And whereas, we the said Julia Steinweg, wife of Henry Steinweg, Sophia Steinweg, wife of Charles Steinweg, Ernestina Steinweg, wife of Henry Steinweg, Junior, and Regina Steinweg, wife of William Steinweg, fully understanding and consenting to all of the terms of said articles of copartnership, a copy of which is hereto attached, and intending, consenting and agreeing, and desirous of having the same carried out in all its parts, for and in the consideration of the sum of one dollar to us each in hand paid, the receipt whereof is herewith acknowledged, and of other considerations hereinafter named, do by these presents covenant and agree to and with the said Henry Steinweg, Charles Steinweg, Henry Steinweg, Jr., and William Steinweg, that in case of the decease of any or either of the copartners of the said firm of Steinweg and Sons, that we and each of us which ever may be left, as the widow of any one or either of the said firm bind ourselves in such event our heirs and assigns to and with the remaining members of said firm by these presents that we or such one of us as shall be left a widow as aforesaid will accept in lieu of any dower interest we or either of us may possess by such decease, the value of the life estate of such of us as may become entitled thereto, as the same shall be ascertained by computation by the tables known in the law as the "Northampton Tables," according to a valuation of said real estate and dower portion, as the same shall be found by Referees appointed for that purpose in the manner following, to wit: One Referee to be named by the said survivors, one by the said widow, who shall agree upon said valuation; and in case of a disagreement by them a third to be selected by said two Referees, in which case a majority of whom shall fix the value of such real estate as aforesaid, so held by the said firm and described aforesaid, or that may be hereafter acquired by the said firm. And that upon the payment thereof of such sum as shall be equal to the life estate therein as aforesaid, ascertained by said Referees and computation upon the value fixed by them and computed from the said Northampton Tables. We the said Sophia, Julia, Ernestina, and Regina Steinweg do covenant and agree to execute and deliver a good and sufficient release or conveyance of said dower right, in and to all of the said real estate now held by the said firm or that may be hereafter acquired by them.

This is the last known photograph of Henry E. Steinway, together with his daughter Doretta and her family. It was taken in Watkins Glen, New York, in 1871, and the family is seated at the base of a cliff, possibly on holiday. Pictured are, from left to right, (first row) Ziegler children Henry Ziegler (who would later succeed C.F. Theodore as Steinway & Sons' chief engineer), Julia Ziegler, and Charles Ziegler; (second row) Mia Lursl, Jacob Ziegler, and Doretta Steinway Ziegler; (third row) Henry E. Steinway. Within months of this photograph, the founder of the greatest piano company in the world would be gone. He died at 74, having mourned the losses of his sons Charles and Henry Jr. and having left the business in the capable hands of his fourth son, William. Henry's wife, Julianne, would live another six years before passing away in 1877.

Two

Henry E. Steinway's Vision
To Build the Best Piano Possible

In his book *People and Pianos*, Steinway's fourth president, Theodore E. Steinway, writes that his paternal grandfather, founder Henry E. Steinway, was "small in physical stature but strong-willed, sturdy, and courageous." He was also doggedly committed to quality. Keenly aware of the growing demand for pianos in his adopted home country, Steinway and his sons threw themselves into experimentation and research in order to produce a piano that would outshine the competition in national and international trade shows and expositions, which were then one of the most important vehicles for marketing and brand-building. Upon the verbal agreement and the $6,000 investment that established Steinway & Sons in 1853, the course was set for a piano firm that would soon eclipse all others in the American and European markets, and technical superiority became a hallmark of the "Steinway System." The following company motto, ascribed to patriarch Henry E. Steinway, is still the credo that drives Steinway's engineers and craftsmen today: "To build the best piano possible." The second generation of Steinways took up the charge. Brothers Henry Jr. and C.F. Theodore, in particular, produced technical and manufacturing innovations that dramatically altered the modern piano—creating an instrument of richer tone and greater mechanical reliability. These advances, combined with the Steinway family's remarkable marketing savvy (including the use of artist endorsements and the opening of a company-owned concert hall that would soon become world-famous), set the stage for massive sales and great wealth by the 1870s.

When the Steinways relocated to New York, 25-year-old Theodore stayed behind in Germany, where he took care of the family's remaining piano business. He maintained a close correspondence with his brothers and, together with Henry Jr., developed the engineering that would revolutionize piano-making and establish the modern piano. Though William pressured Theodore to come to America, he resisted—his wife, Johanna, abhorred New York. As a result, the Steinway brothers' creative processes are well documented through the letters passing between Theodore and Henry Jr. Between 1853 and 1865, they shared notes, drawings, specifications, and calculations that would create the foundation for the most innovative piano patents developed by Steinway & Sons. After the death of both Henry Jr. and Charles in 1865, William finally persuaded Theodore to join him in New York to help run Steinway & Sons as head of the technical department. Theodore sold the remaining family business in Brunswick and moved to New York—but this would not be the final chapter in the story of Steinway & Sons in Germany.

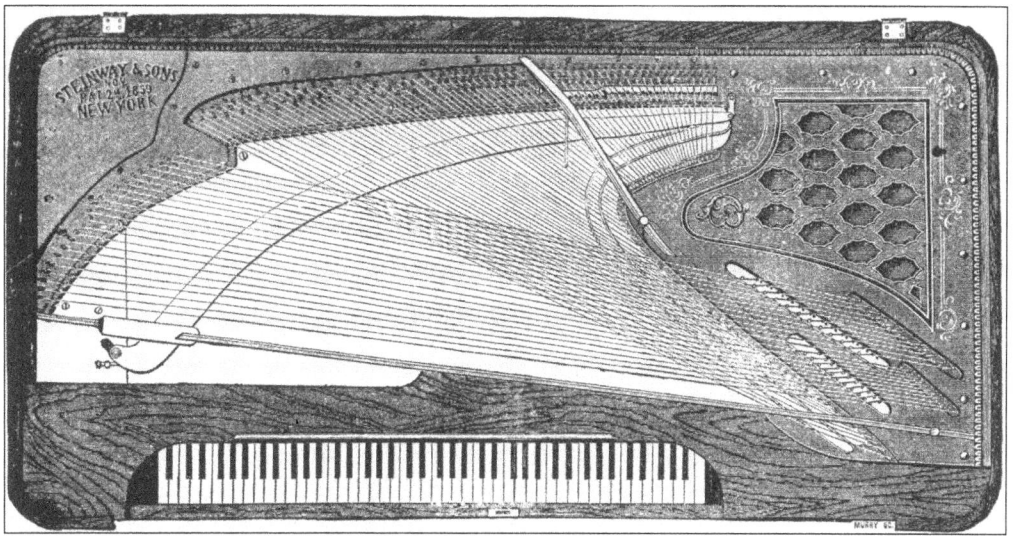

The "overstrung scale" was the brainchild of Henry Steinway Jr. He was not the first engineer to try it, but in 1859, he was the first to perfect it. In an overstrung scale, the piano's bass strings are fitted in a tier above the treble and middle strings to allow for a longer bass string length and to draw the bridges into the soundboard's center, where the vibrations are of greater amplitude.

Style 2.—7 OCTAVES—ROSEWOOD.
Large front round corners; ogee moulding; richly carved legs and lyre;
Patent agraffe treble.
Length, 6 feet 8 inches; width, 3 feet 4 inches.
This Piano may be had with additional Serpentine Moulding around lower edge of case, at $25 extra.

Early pianos produced by Steinway & Sons were square. Two years after the founding of the company, in 1855, the Steinways exhibited an overstrung square piano at the American Institute fair at New York's legendary Crystal Palace and nabbed first prize, a gold medal. But by 1888, square pianos were phased out of the Steinway catalog.

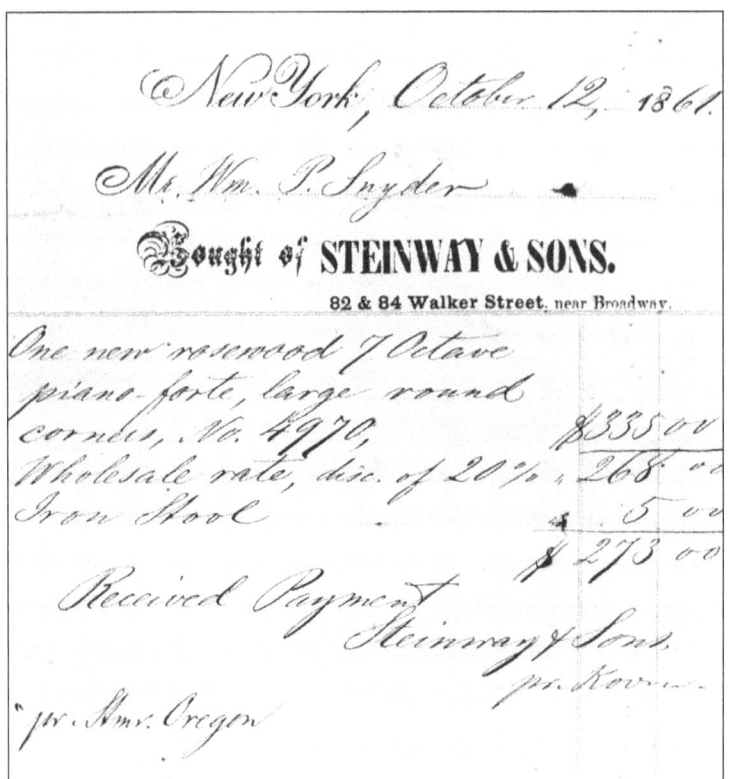

Steinway sales were robust by 1861. This receipt for a new rosewood seven-octave piano shows a purchase price of $273. The sale took place at the Steinway & Sons Walker Street facility just two months after Charles G. Steinway returned from service in the Civil War as part of New York's 5th Regiment.

Awards were a mainstay of Steinway & Sons' promotions in the early years. In 1867, the company was awarded this medal at the Paris Exposition, touching off a marketing skirmish between Steinway and its primary American competitor, Chickering, which was also awarded prizes. In 1989, a glass case at Steinway Hall in Manhattan was smashed, and the Paris medal, along with several others, was stolen. It was never recovered.

STEINWAY & SONS.

FIRST PRIZE MEDAL.

Great International Exhibition,

LONDON, 1862,

FOR POWERFUL, CLEAR, BRILLIANT, AND SYMPATHETIC TONE, WITH EXCELLENCE OF WORKMANSHIP,

AS SHOWN IN GRAND AND SQUARE PIANOS.

There were two hundred and sixty-nine Pianos, from all parts of the world, entered for competition, and the special correspondent of the *Times* says:

"Messrs. STEINWAY's indorsement by the Jurors is emphatic, and stronger, and more to the point than that of any European maker."

This greatest triumph of American Pianofortes in England has caused a sensation in musical circles throughout the Continent, and, as a result, the Messrs. STEINWAY are in constant receipt of orders from Europe, thus inaugurating a new phase in the history of American Pianofortes, *by creating in them an article of export.*

In the midst of the Civil War, Steinway & Sons entered two square pianos and two grands in London's Great International Exhibition, attended by more than six million people. Steinway pianos made a huge splash among the attendees and did well among American competitors, but the family had hoped for more recognition among the international judges. Nevertheless, following this exhibition in 1862, Steinway pianos dominated the American market. Most other piano manufacturers were openly copying the Steinway System, which later became known as simply the "American System." The early success of the company is often attributed to the Steinways' close collaboration among family members and the fact that each brother brought a particular skill set—whether in engineering, artistry, marketing, or administration—to the table. The 1860s would bring personal losses and financial hardships that would sorely test this recipe for success.

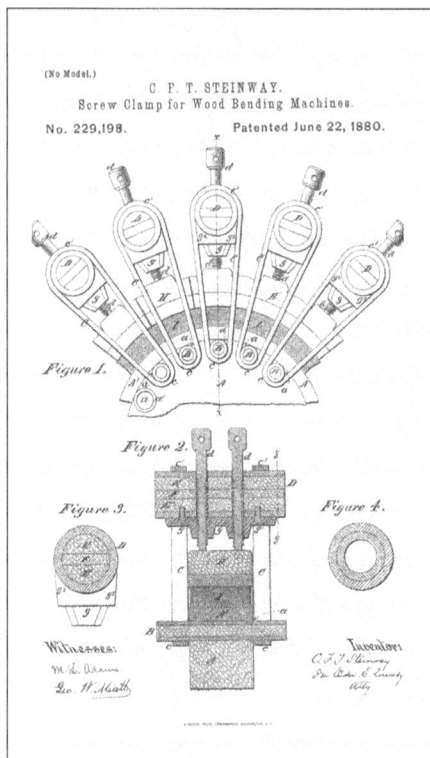

Another great Theodore Steinway technical innovation was the process for building the Steinway grand piano rim. In 1880, he developed and patented a screw clamp that formed the basis for a wood-bending machine strong enough to create the curved grand piano rim. The rim-bending process for Steinway grand pianos is followed today virtually unchanged from Theodore's design: a foot-wide "book" of 17-ply glued hard-rock maple is clamped into place in the rim press, where it is bent into close to a 90-degree angle. This dramatic process, choreographed by a team of four to five men and depicted in the 1908 photograph below, is today one of the highlights of the Steinway & Sons factory tour experience. Theodore was incredibly productive; at least 45 of Steinway's 139 patents were the result of his ideas.

This square Steinway piano, built in 1854, is the second-oldest known manufactured piano (Steinway & Sons serial No. 521) and is the oldest working piano in the United States. It was sold in January 1855 to dealer J.T. Hammick of Catskill. A similar 1858 piano is on display at the La Guardia and Wagner Archives at La Guardia Community College in Long Island City, New York.

The Steinway piano factory on Fifty-Third Street, built in 1860, was designed by architect Louis Berger and cost $150,000 to construct. This curious photograph, assembled by a creative spirit, is a composite view of the workday made by cutting and pasting photographs of workers onto a drawing of the Steinway factory interior. Charles G. Steinway is seated in the front row.

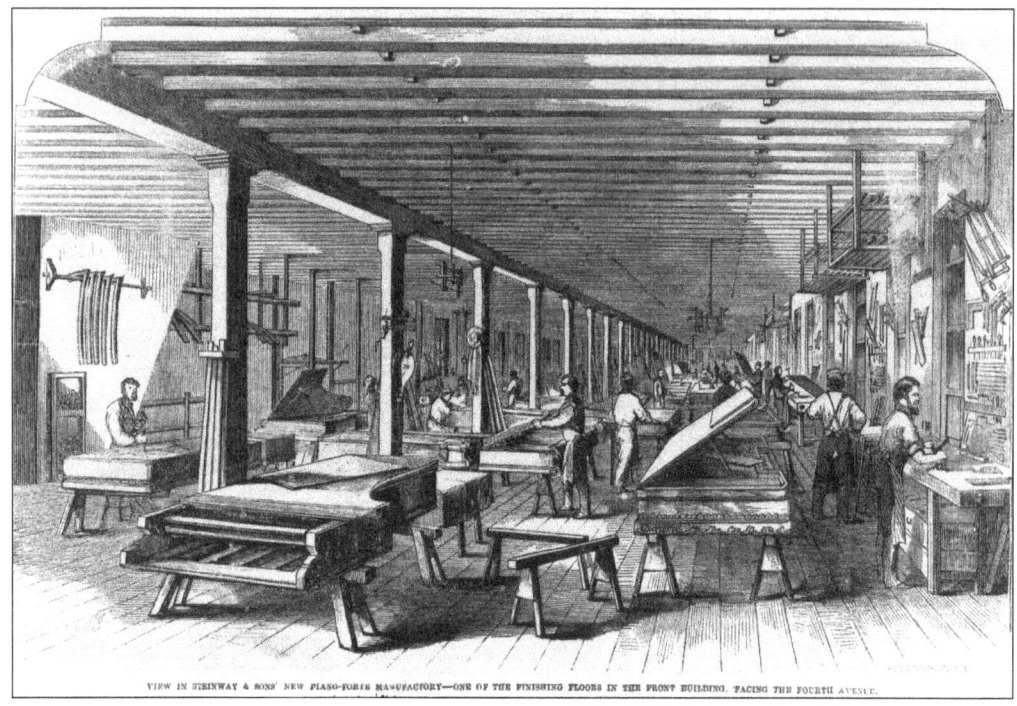

This 1860 lithograph of the new Steinway & Sons factory on Fifty-Third Street was published in *Frank Leslie's Weekly*. It depicts work underway in one of the finishing rooms in the factory's front building, facing Fourth Avenue, now Park Avenue. Founder Henry E. Steinway himself oversaw the construction of this state-of-the-art, 175,000-square-foot facility.

In 1866, William Steinway oversaw the construction of the company's first concert hall, which, at 2,000 seats, was to be the second largest in Manhattan. Steinway Hall, on Fourteenth Street near the Academy of Music, was soon to become the center of the music world in New York City. This building was the first of three New York Steinway Halls constructed to date. The adjacent house at 107 East Fourteenth Street was the home of William Steinway.

This lithograph, taken from *Frank Leslie's Weekly*, illustrates an elegant sales showroom at Steinway Hall. The first floor of Steinway Hall was made up of sales rooms for square and upright pianos, while the second floor housed even larger sales rooms filled with additional uprights and grands.

Around 1870, Steinway & Sons started marketing the "boudoir" piano as a step further into the growing upright market. This piano, five feet wide and less than four feet high, had a detachable front portion that enabled the action, keyboard, legs, and feet to be removed from the piano's case. It proved a popular model for those seeking a smaller, more portable piano.

When Steinway expanded its operations to Queens, its first facility was on Riker Avenue on Bowery Bay. This site housed a sawmill, iron and brass foundries, and metalworks. Parts made here were shipped across the East River to the Fifty-Third Street factory for assembly. A primary motivator for William's decision to expand to Queens was to remove workers from the influence of New York City, where labor unions and worker unrest had become a growing challenge. Above is a group of foundry workers at the Rikers plant in 1885; the man in the derby hat is a foreman. Below is a group of men in the leg department; the men are holding legs and a lyre for a square piano, a grand piano leg, a saw, a rim component, and a soundboard bridge. At their feet is a glue pot with a whisk broom.

The second Queens Steinway facility was constructed about a mile from the original buildings at Rikers. This new 125,000-square-foot facility was built by Steinway's second president, Charles H. Steinway (son of Charles G.), who took the helm following William's death in 1896. Steinway had bounced back from near bankruptcy toward the end of the century, and by 1901, when this factory was built, it was turning a record profit. A series of photographs taken in 1908 shows the new Ditmars factory bustling with activity. Above, young boys work to assemble the piano's action parts. Child labor reform was not widespread in the United States until 1938. Below, workers in the foundry clean plate castings.

The production of upright pianos had been a point of some contention between brothers William, Henry Jr., and Theodore in the 1850s and 1860s. Theodore was all for designing a modern upright and tried to persuade his brothers to embrace it, but William and Henry Jr. were skeptical, preferring to keep the focus of Steinway & Sons on high-end grand pianos. Thus the company did not make its first upright piano until 1862, and then under some reluctance on the parts of William and Henry. But there was no denying that the upright piano was growing in demand in both Europe and America. Theodore's sophisticated engineering helped bring an upright piano that met the Steinway requirements for sound, tone, and durability into production. By the turn of the century, Steinway upright pianos were a mainstay of each year's catalog. These workers in 1908 are fitting actions into upright pianos.

Fredrick C. Rathgeber was a superintendent at the Queens factories from 1872 until his death in 1922. He worked under Steinway's second president, Charles H. Steinway, a shrewd fiscal conservative who teamed up with his brother Fred and their cousin Henry Ziegler to form the third generation of Steinway leadership.

These factory workers are, from left to right, S.H. Lesh, Fred Speyrer, W. Scully, and C. Lawson. Months after this photograph was taken at the Ditmars plant in 1908, Charles H. Steinway sold the Fifty-Third Street factory in Manhattan for $650,000. All New York Steinway manufacturing facilities were then located in Queens, and they remain so today.

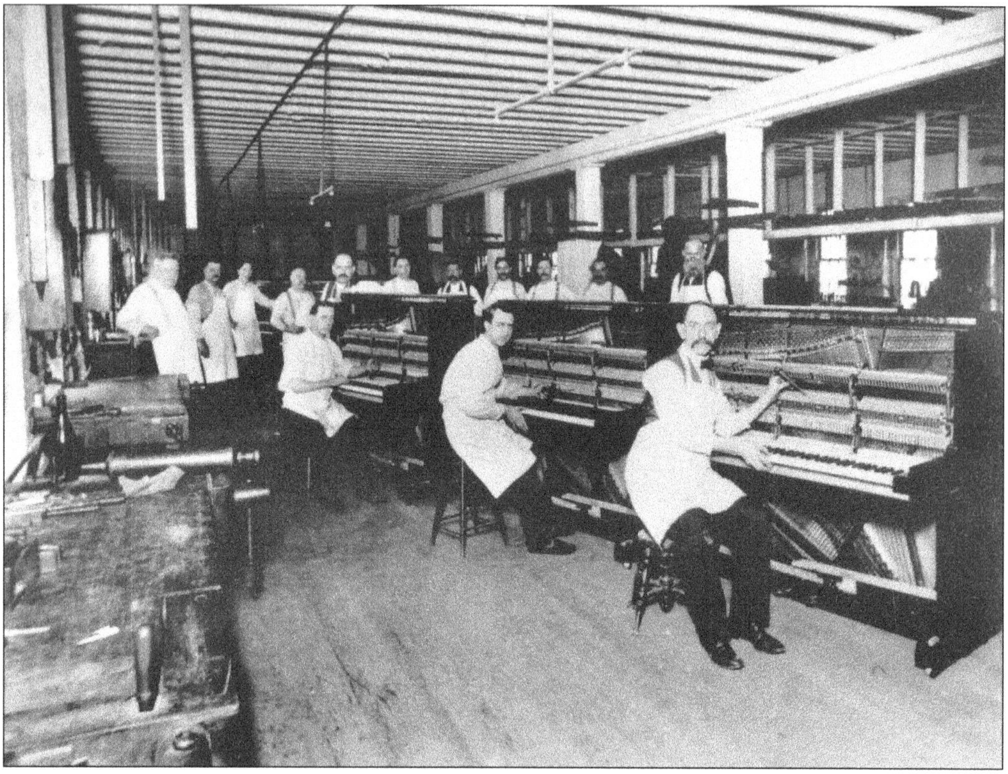

Steinway craftsmen in this image are "voicing" pianos in 1908. They are adjusting and balancing various parts of the piano's action to elicit a particular sound from the piano, thus imbuing each instrument with its own unique personality. Voicing is one of the last departments each Steinway piano visits before it is shipped from the factory.

This worker at the Steinway Ditmars plant, photographed around 1922, demonstrates the new use of a rotary sander to "skin off" the piano's hammer heads, one at a time. This removes any dirt or grease to prevent compromise to the hammer. Note the "whoopee" hat, made from a man's carved-up felt fedora.

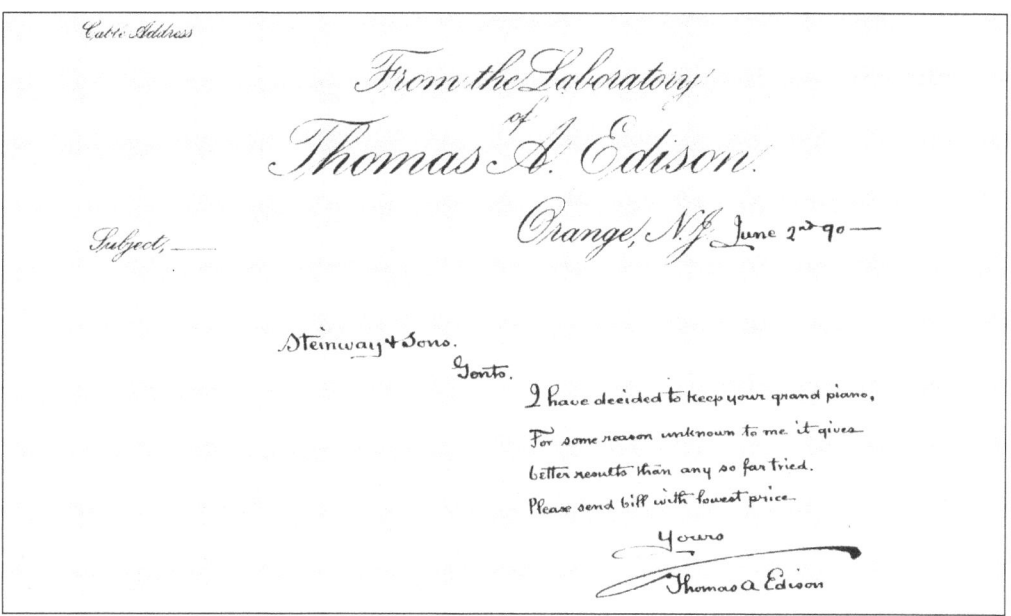

By the late 1800s, Steinway's name was renowned, and the company's fan base was growing. This letter from Thomas Edison, written in 1890 and addressed from Orange, New Jersey, expresses Edison's request for a bill to cover the piano he had been evidently trying out. This was the same year that Edison established the Edison General Electric Company, later known simply as GE.

Steinway & Sons also dabbled in enterprises other than piano manufacturing. In 1888, William Steinway entered into an agreement with Gottlieb Daimler to manufacture Daimler engines and, subsequently, established a franchise for the Daimler Motor Company of America. Although Daimler engines were for a time displayed in the showrooms of Steinway Hall on Fourteenth Street, it was not a financially fruitful endeavor for Steinway.

FRONT VIEW OF STEINWAY HALL
and **Pianoforte Warerooms**, with adjoining building, containing the Office. Nos. 107, 109 & 111 East 14th Street, extending through to 15th Street, between Union Square and the Academy of Music, **NEW YORK.**

REAR VIEW OF STEINWAY HALL
on 15th Street, extending through from 14th Street, with the adjoining building, containing the artists' rooms in the upper stories, and the piano shipping and delivery office on the first floor. **NEW YORK.**

STEINWAY HALL
with Concert Room and Steinway & Sons' Pianoforte Warerooms, with the adjoining building, containing the Office, Nos. 15 & 17 Lower Seymour St., near Portman Square, W.,
LONDON, England.

STEINWAY'S PIANOFABRIK.
Steinway & Sons' Branch Piano Factory and Warerooms, St. Pauli, Neue Rosenstrasse, Nos. 20, 21, 22, 23 and 24,
HAMBURG, Germany.

This extensive establishment was founded by Steinway & Sons in 1880, in order to properly supply the large and constantly growing demand for Steinway pianos throughout Europe, and to prepare the instruments for the humid European climate, Hamburg being a free port and unrivaled point of distribution.

This 1879 advertisement proudly showcases Steinway's manufacturing and sales facilities, including front and rear views of Steinway Hall, Fourteenth Street, New York City; Steinway Hall, Lower Seymour Street, London; and the Hamburg factory, which was to open the following year. The facility in Hamburg, known as "Schanzenstrasse," was built in 1880 to supply pianos for European and other export markets. Theodore had long yearned to return to Germany, and his brother William eventually saw the benefit in opening a finishing plant in Hamburg to serve the European market. With the construction of this facility, after nearly 30 years, the Steinway family would again manufacture pianos in Germany. Steinway's *Pianofabrik* in Hamburg purchased parts from New York, assembled them, and shipped finished pianos to England. The factory pictured above was bombed and destroyed in 1943. William R. Steinway, grandson of founder Henry E. Steinway, worked at this factory before World War II.

William R. Steinway stands in the lumberyards at the Hamburg factory in 1925. "Uncle Billie," as he was known, chose his German love, Mariechen Kiesler, over the opportunity to become president of Steinway & Sons in New York. Upon his decision to follow Marie to her German village to marry her, William's cousin Fred declared, "Well, that's it. You'll never be president of Steinway." Billie fired back, "The hell with it."

In this photograph, a group of Steinway dealers is gathered for a meeting and luncheon on the steps of the beautiful Claremont Inn in 1914. The inn was located at the north end of the oval formed by Riverside Drive, forking just below Grant's Tomb. The inn was demolished in 1951.

William Steinway, the son of founder Henry E. Steinway, was the indisputable leader of the company until his death in 1896, shepherding Steinway & Sons from a small family venture to its status as the manufacturers of the finest pianos in the world. He was a powerhouse of authority, business acumen, social networking, philanthropy, marketing creativity, and fiscal administration. He was also a passionate romantic and suffered intense heartbreak at the hands of his first wife, Regina, whose extramarital affairs eventually fractured the family and sent Regina back to Germany with her son Alfred, progeny of an illegitimate union with a neighbor. With Regina, William had two children, George and Paula. The family, including Regina's son Alfred, are pictured above. Even after her admission of the affair and her departure with little Alfred for Germany, William pined for Regina. When she returned her wedding ring to him, with "a few affectionate and poignant words," he recorded in his diary, "I again break down and sob as though my heart would break."

Three

WEALTH, POWER, AND PRESTIGE
A LEGACY TAKES SHAPE

Steinway & Sons' triumphs in piano engineering, and the accompanying swell in sales, created a life of wealth and prestige for the family. By the 1870s, the Steinways were well known in New York society, particularly Henry E. Steinway's fourth son, William, who served as the company's first president. William was arguably the most Americanized of the second generation of Steinways. He adapted well to life in New York and gravitated to positions of leadership, both inside and outside of the family business. A close friend of Grover Cleveland, William Steinway was active in Democratic politics, sat on the boards of banks, and came to play a critical role in New York City transportation and the development of modern-day Astoria. With affable William known colloquially as "Mr. Music" in New York's high society, the Steinway family enjoyed decades of leisure and comfort at the end of the 19th century. From the beginning, and until the 1970s, the Steinways maintained deliberate and careful control of the leadership of the firm, keeping the presidency in the hands of a trusted son or nephew and keeping all technical and manufacturing intelligence closely guarded. This insular protection of the firm led to the creation of an iconic brand mystique and the development of a family legacy like few others in American history.

Henry W.T. Steinway (left) and Frederick Theodore Steinway (right) were the first and third sons of Charles G. and the grandsons of founder Henry E. Steinway. While they appear amiable in this photograph, taken around 1888, their relationship was strained, largely due to Henry W.T.'s resentment toward Frederick and their middle brother, Charles H. Of the three brothers, eldest Henry W.T. was the only one who would not later assume the Steinway presidency. He was reported as fractious, entitled, and haughty, and he made no secret of his resistance to take orders from his uncle William. From 1885 to 1891, the relationships between Henry W.T. and the other Steinway men deteriorated beyond repair; he was forced to resign from the company on New Year's Eve 1891. He responded with three angry lawsuits against Steinway & Sons, each charging business transgressions and fiscal mismanagement that he claimed were costing all the Steinways money. Though he lost all three suits, Henry W.T. maintained his anger against the family—even while living off the dividends of his Steinway stock—until his death in 1939.

The first Steinway Hall opened in 1866, housing over 100 pianos and an auditorium of 2,500 seats. Steinway Hall became New York City's artistic cultural center and home of the New York Philharmonic until Carnegie Hall opened in 1891. The introduction of Steinway Hall to New York City was a cornerstone achievement of William Steinway's presidency.

This street-level view of Steinway Hall was taken around 1910. To the right can be seen the construction of the Fourteenth Street elevated train. Steinway Hall recast Steinway & Sons as more than a piano manufacturer—the company became known as a champion for music and a destination for artists and piano enthusiasts the world over. Steinway Hall's successor at Fifty-Seventh Street, constructed in 1925, would build upon this foundation.

Cultural highlights at Steinway Hall included Victoria Woodhull campaigning for the women's rights movement in 1872 and performances by virtuoso musicians, including Fritz Kreisler, Walter Damrosch, and Anton Rubinstein. Charles Dickens gave 22 readings at Steinway Hall between December 1867 and April 1868.

"Everybody is delighted with the acoustic qualities," wrote William Steinway in his diary after the opening of his new concert hall. "House is filled to overflowing. Great success." In 1877, Steinway Hall was the site of a demonstration of how sound can be transmitted via telephone wire. Rapt onlookers watched as music from a Steinway was transmitted from Philadelphia to Steinway Hall.

In this illustration, based on a lithograph by artist Amédée de Noé, attendees of the 1867 Paris Exposition are crazed in their enthusiasm for the piano played by Desiré Magnus. The image represents the rapidly growing enthusiasm for the American piano; the piano "mania" depicted here would set the stage for Steinway's success in the American piano market. (Courtesy New York Public Library.)

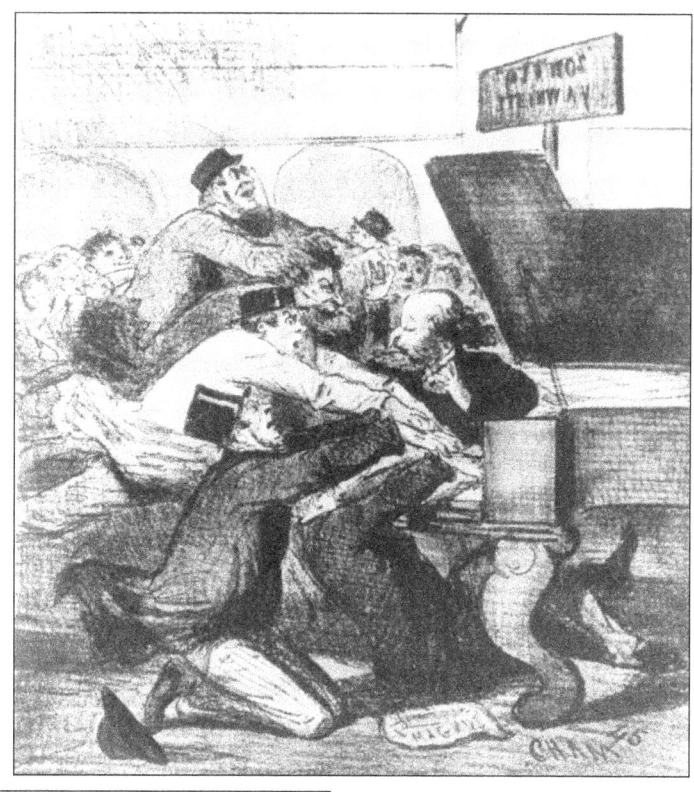

Nine years later, in 1876, Steinway was continuing to dominate the piano market and the hearts of music enthusiasts around the world. This lithograph depicts Steinway's "Piano-forte" exhibit at the United States' Centennial Exhibition in Philadelphia. The exhibit was built by Doretta Steinway's husband, Jacob Ziegler. Displayed on the wall is the "Highest Award" to Steinway, as well as two medals of honor and two diplomas of merit.

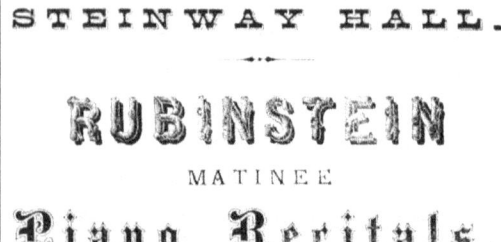

Early in company history, Steinway & Sons paired the creation of exceptional-quality pianos with savvy marketing strategies, including the cultivation of relationships with virtuoso pianists to endorse the Steinway piano. In 1872, William Steinway brought the acclaimed Russian Anton Rubinstein to America for a 215-stop tour. The tour was enormously successful, and the publicity for Steinway was massive. The Steinway Artist, a pianist who has chosen to perform exclusively on Steinway pianos, was born.

This caricature by Joseph Keppler illustrates the popularity of the powerhouse Rubinstein during his performances at Steinway Hall. Rubinstein's fellow performers are Theodore Thomas, upper left; Carlotta Patti, second from left; and Henri Weiniawski, next to Rubinstein, holding a violin. At Rubinstein's Steinway Hall debut, 3,000 people pushed into a concert hall intended for 2,500.

In 1891, young Polish virtuoso Ignacy Jan Paderewski was the next big name invited by Steinway to America. He was managed by Charles Tretbar, head of Steinway's relatively new of Concert & Artist Department. William had seen the success of the Rubinstein tour and what it had done for piano sales, and he was eager to repeat the phenomenon. Steinway sent Paderewski on a grueling national tour of 107 concerts over 117 days. Though fatigued and dealing with an injured finger, Paderewski rallied to repeat the tour the following year, this time completing 80 performances in the first six months of 1892. The young star rocketed to international celebrity. He remained a close associate of Steinway's artist managers, especially the legendary Ernest Urchs, until Paderewski's death in 1939, long after the famed pianist had become a renowned diplomat, statesman, and philanthropist. The photograph below depicts Paderewski at his Steinway piano in 1892.

PADEREWSKI AT HIS FAVORITE PIANO

By the 1870s, the Steinway family was indisputably wealthy. William Steinway would become a millionaire in 1881, one of only 400 in New York. The Steinway mansion was the family's summer home in the late 19th century. William purchased the estate from ophthalmologist Benjamin T. Pike Jr. in 1870 for $125,500. As of this writing, the mansion is still standing east of Steinway Street, near the East River.

William married his second wife, Elizabeth Ranft, in 1880. By this time, his two children, George and Paula, from his first marriage to Regina were 15 and 14. William was wealthy, powerful, and soon to be the father of three more children. His second marriage seemed lacking in the passion of his first, however, with historians describing Elizabeth as "dour." She would bear two sons and a daughter and die at 40.

From left to right, Frederick T. Steinway, Henry W.T. Steinway, George A. Steinway, and Constantin Schmidt are pictured above relaxing on the porch of the Steinway mansion around 1888. The network of cousins in the Steinway family was an important support system to the business. Constantin Schmidt was married to Julia Ziegler, the daughter of Doretta Steinway and the granddaughter of founder Henry E. Steinway. Julia's sister Louisa Ziegler married a man named Henry Cassebeer, and both the Schmidt and Cassebeer families would yield important players—mostly male—who would change the course of Steinway history. In the image below, Frederick Steinway, Henry W.T. Steinway, Julia Z. Schmidt, Constantin Schmidt, and George A. Steinway pose from left to right.

The wealthy and prominent Steinway family was a magnet for social engagements, and the Astoria mansion made a smart setting for gatherings and parties. Here, members of the family play croquet with friends including toy magnate F.A.O. Schwarz, a close friend of William's. (William's diary makes mention of visits with Schwarz and of "drinking fine beer" with his friend.) Pictured are, from left to right, Julia Ziegler Schmidt, Henry Cassebeer, George A. Steinway, Charles H. Steinway, F.A.O. Schwarz, Marie Steinway, Ida Schwarz, Frederick T. Steinway, and Henry W.T. Steinway. In the photograph at left, F.A.O. Schwarz sits with Henrietta (center) and Ida Schwarz.

In the mid-1880s, William Steinway's two sons from his marriage to Elizabeth are pictured on the porch of the Steinway mansion, possibly with their governess. These two boys—William R. "Billie" on the left and Theodore E. on the right—possessed greatly differing temperaments. Billie was confident and outgoing and seemed a natural to take on the leadership of Steinway & Sons as he grew older. Theodore was artistic and moody and given to isolationism. He loved theater and took pride in the fact that his middle initial, E, was an homage to the great actor Edwin Booth. Ironically, it was Theodore who ultimately accepted the role of the Steinway presidency, albeit with great reluctance. And it was Theodore who was left with the unenviable challenge of shepherding Steinway & Sons through the Great Depression and into the war years.

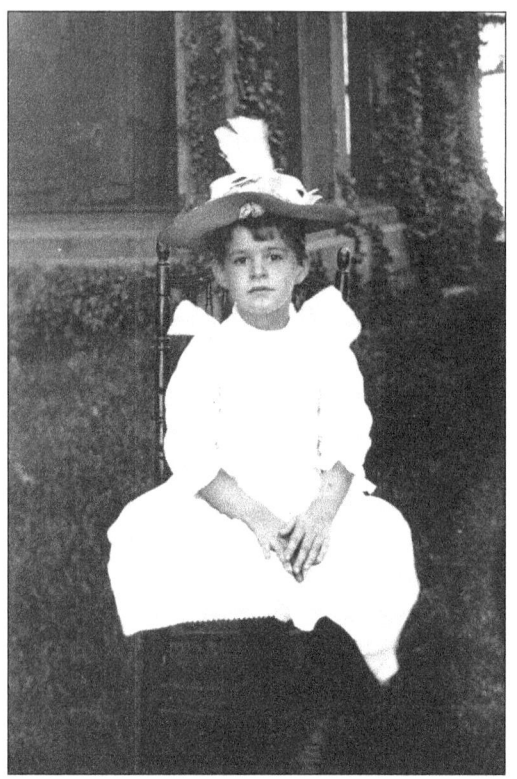

Maude Steinway was the third child of William Steinway and his second wife, Elizabeth. She was only four years old when her mother died suddenly of Bright's disease (now commonly known as nephritis). Her older half-sister Paula stepped in to help raise Maude and older brothers William R. and Theodore E., the latter of whom would eventually become Steinway's fourth president. Maude Steinway Paige died in New York City in 1976.

From left to right, Paul Schmidt, Henry Arthur Cassebeer, and Herman Schmidt sit on the front steps of the Steinway mansion around 1888. Arthur Cassebeer later went to Harvard and became a doctor. He was the first member of the extended Steinway family to go to college. As an adult, Paul Schmidt became assistant to his uncle Frederick T. Steinway during the latter's presidency of Steinway & Sons.

The Steinway mansion was a luxurious gathering point for Steinways and their guests, and it boasted an extensive domestic staff. The group above is the crew servicing the greenhouse and grounds. The mansion was named to the National Register of Historic Places in 1983. It is located at 18–33 Forty-First Street, Astoria, New York City.

The Windsor Arcade, an early version of a shopping mall, stood at the corner of Fifth Avenue and Forty-Sixth Street for 10 years, from 1901 to 1911. The building was a three-story Beaux-Arts complex of shops and galleries, including a Steinway & Sons retail showroom. The store is pictured here around 1901.

C.F. Theodore Steinway is pictured at his home in Braunschweig, Germany, with two unidentified women around 1885. In 1880, after years in New York, Theodore returned to Germany to open a Steinway factory that would buy parts from Steinway's New York operation and provide the European market with finished pianos.

One of the richest sources of Steinway history is the remarkable diary of William Steinway. The nine volumes of his personal journal, comprising some 2,500 pages, span the years 1861 to 1896, with the last entry made just a few weeks before his death. William recorded everything—from business dealings and family gatherings to coded references to his own sex life. The diary is on display at the Smithsonian Museum in Washington, DC, and has been completely digitized through the Smithsonian's Online William Steinway Diary Project.

Four

Craft and Creativity
The Rise of the Steinway Artisan

Seven years after the company's founding, Steinway & Sons opened a new state-of-the-art factory in New York City. At the opening celebration in 1860, guests were treated to a tour of the new facility, during which they were provided the opportunity to watch some of Steinway's 300 workers crafting and assembling parts in the various departments that would collectively create the now-famous Steinway piano. The factory tour is a tradition that continues today at the company's Astoria factory. Starting in the lumberyard, visitors are taken on a two-hour walking tour of the historic facility to observe workers as they create and assemble the various parts of the piano: rim, case, soundboard, bridge, action, and more. These workers—many of whom are second- or third-generation Steinway employees—are part of the tradition of skilled artisans without which Steinway & Sons could never have built its impressive legacy. The Steinway artisan is a gifted—and historically powerful—worker, imbued with extensive manufacturing experience and an artist's sensitivity to quality and beauty. Steinway pianos are built by hand and always have been, as Theodore E. Steinway observed in his book *People and Pianos*: "Machine work was substituted for hand work only in the relatively few operations where quality would not be affected in the slightest—a policy which has never been modified. Even so, the power-driven tool must still be guided by the hand of a man." In its first decades of operation, Steinway's reliance on skilled artisans was both a hallmark of its success and an Achilles heel; when skilled workers organized, William Steinway had trouble.

Steinway & Sons was founded not by a businessman but by a talented piano-builder, and the company has always placed a premium on the identification and cultivation of craftsmen capable of creating the world's finest pianos, one at a time, by hand. The Steinway artisan is a highly skilled master, often possessing decades of experience in one area of piano-building. In 1858, Steinway's New York factory employed 100 workers. By 1925, that figure had skyrocketed to 2,300. The number of employees working at Steinway & Sons was to rise and fall dramatically through the decades, as the company dealt with booms, busts, strikes, recessions, and wartime closures. In this photograph taken in 1916 at the Ditmars factory in Queens, a worker "needles" the piano's hammers to regulate its tone. The same time-honored voicing process is still in use today.

As far back as 1859, Steinway had to contend with unionizing workers and cries for wage increases, among other demands. The different presidents of Steinway & Sons had different approaches to the issue—and some were much more willing than others to negotiate with union representatives. The workers in this 1908 photograph are at work in the grand rim department.

In the 1860s, Steinway struggled with a shortage of skilled labor, and a series of strikes over the following several decades meant that William, as well as Charles and Frederick later, was frequently at the mercy of the talented tradesmen who were becoming increasingly confident in their own value. Here, men work on plate finishing in the early 1900s.

At the turn of the century, Steinway & Sons was prospering, reporting a $420,000 profit in 1899. The construction of the second Queens factory at Ditmars meant a corresponding increase in labor. These grand bellymen, pictured in 1908, are, from left to right, Carl Petterson, Anders Wallman, Otto Bredow, Charles Kovarik, and J.A. Kullberg. Many Steinway workers in the early days were German immigrants.

These varnishers are, from left to right, Walter Morris, Joseph Schaub, Joseph Rebb, William Novak, Louis Altendorfer, Karl Brisch, and David Morris. At the end of the 1800s, piano varnishers were among the craftsmen most successful in striking for higher wages and better working conditions. Varnishers, or "rubbers," had a very difficult job requiring intense brawn and endurance—and pianos could not be completed without them.

In 1923, a total of 1,500 workers were building pianos at Steinway & Sons, and two years later, that number had climbed to 2,300. But hard times were looming—after 1929, piano shipments nationwide would drop by about 90 percent. In 1932, Steinway sold only around 900 pianos. No matter the quantity produced, however, every Steinway piano goes through the same meticulous manufacturing process. Once the grand piano's rim is complete, it moves to the casemaking department, where it is fitted with internal braces and a keybed. Embellishments, carvings, and decorations are begun at this point. In the photograph above, workers in the leg department pose around 1908. Below, men work on carving upper panel frames.

It is unclear why so many violins hang in the factory's carving department in this photograph from 1908. At left is William Bernauer, a Steinway personnel director. Three decades later, in 1939, Bernauer and paymaster Joe Pirola stood at the local public school while workers lined up to vote for or against joining the United Piano Workers Union, Local No. 102. Bernauer's and Pirola's presence was intended to ensure that all men casting a vote were indeed employees of Steinway & Sons. The union was voted in, and then-president Theodore E. Steinway took it personally, expressing intense frustration that his workers organized "against" him. The adoption of Local No. 102 marked a milestone in a back-and-forth battle between Steinway and its workforce that traced its roots back as far as 1872.

The process of casting the one-piece iron frame for Steinway pianos is arduous and dangerous. First the iron is cast into a mold; later, it is removed, cooled, ground, and finished in preparation for its starring role as the support for the piano's strings. In these images from 1908, Steinway craftsmen create the frame's mold and the frame itself at the Queens factory-based foundry. The cast-iron frame is incredibly strong and can withstand enormous string tension, thus creating the powerful sound for which Steinway pianos are known. Unprotected foundry work is damaging to respiration. In the 1930s, following a spate of silicosis cases in the state of New York, Steinway began outsourcing its cast-iron plate production, marking the first time that the company did not manufacture every part of the piano on-site. In 1999, Steinway purchased the O.S. Kelly Foundry and brought plate production back in-house (though at a different physical location) for the first time in nearly six decades.

C5110-5—Grand case making department.

A case cornice is being glued into the piano's case at the Steinway Ditmars factory. The hard-rock maple rim has been planed and perfected and is now with the casemakers, who will create and install the rest of the instrument's cabinetry. The case houses nearly all of the Steinway piano's 12,000 parts.

In finishing the top side of the plate, a coat of "japan"—a thick varnish—was applied, as depicted in this photograph from 1916. The coated plate then had to be baked hard in the specially designed ovens at the rear. Japanning preps the plate for its final coating of bronze lacquer.

These workers are gluing ivory onto piano keys. Ivory was commonly used in piano keys until the mid-1950s, when Steinway and other American piano manufacturers moved to using plastic.

C5110-8—Gluing Ivory on Piano Keys.

C5110-S—Spinning copper wire on Bass strings.

These workers manage a machine designed for wrapping a copper winding around steel piano strings. Steinway strings must withstand enormous tension, and over the years, the company has experimented with various string materials including soft iron and hard steel, with or without the copper covering process shown in this image.

C5110-W—Pattern and scale draughting Room.

Company president Theodore E. Steinway (left) and his cousin Theodore Cassebeer are pictured here in the pattern room at the Ditmars factory in 1916. On the far wall are portraits of Henry E. and Julianne Steinway. The open door on the right enters into a closet in which were kept scale drawings of pianos.

These craftsmen are stringing upright backs. The Steinway upright piano is built using the same materials, conditioning processes, techniques, and skilled craftsmen as the Steinway grand. The man in the foreground is tapping down tuning pins. The man to the left in the background is possibly Max Neubert, a longtime factory foreman.

C4741-E—Upright stringing Department.

In 1916, when this photograph was taken, Steinway sales topped $1.1 million. But booms and busts in the piano market had a cruel impact on the fate of the Steinway workforce. In the early 1930s, thousands of workers were furloughed, and most were never hired back. For five years, the factory was run by a skeleton crew of part-time workers.

C4741-H—Upright action regulating Department.

The rim of the grand piano must be exceedingly strong. It supports the weight of the soundboard and the frame. The Steinway rim is made of many layers of laminated wood that are glued and bent in a dramatic process developed and honed by C.F. Theodore Steinway in the 1870s. The process has been fundamentally unchanged for well over a century.

After the outbreak of war in 1914, and after the passage of child labor laws that saw the removal of children from the piano-making workforce, women began working for hourly wages at the Steinway factory. They were mostly employed in the action department, where they took on the fine work of producing and assembling the intricate mechanisms that drive the piano's hammers against its strings to produce sound. The action for one Steinway piano key is made up of over 57 parts, and Steinway is the only American piano manufacturer that still builds all its own action parts. These women, pictured around 1950, work on grand piano action assemblies.

Five

STEINWAY VILLAGE
THE COMPANY COMES TO ASTORIA

The story of Steinway in New York recounts an unusual but not unknown phenomenon—that of the "company town" that becomes, over time, an intrinsic part of a community. In 1870, Steinway & Sons needed a solution to two challenges. First, business was booming, and the company needed additional manufacturing facilities to meet the demand for its pianos. Second, organized labor was gathering steam, and William Steinway needed a strategy to separate his workers from the influence of union agitation. He began by purchasing large swaths of farmland in the northern end of what is now Long Island City, and upon this land he built Steinway's new lumber mill and foundry. Construction of additional factory facilities in the area would soon follow. The next step was to establish housing and community services for Steinway's workers. Following a wave of strikes in the 1870s, other American industrialists followed similar plans; company-owned housing gave employers leverage over employees, who could be evicted or foreclosed upon in the event of disruptive labor protests. By this time, some 400 workers were employed by Steinway & Sons in Queens making parts that were then shipped across the East River to the Manhattan factory for assembly. These workers needed housing, roads, schools, churches, and utilities. Steinway & Sons was more than willing to oblige, and the company's contributions shaped a neighborhood roughly encompassing the area that is today bounded by Bowery Bay to the north and Ditmars Boulevard to the south, between Thirty-First and Hazen Streets. Colloquially, this region is still known as "Steinway."

William Steinway bankrolled a power plant, a firehouse, a post office, a church, a library, and a kindergarten for the residents of his company town in Astoria, which was eventually called simply Steinway, even by the US Post Office. By 1895, the year before William died, around 7,000 people lived in the village, many of them employees at the Steinway & Sons factory. Steinway even paid a portion of the kindergarten teacher's salary. A few of the children in this 1911 Steinway Village kindergarten photograph have been identified. They are as follows: Peter Schumann (the boy leaning against the fence in the dark suit); Charles Roeckell (the boy in the sailor suit); and Catherine Schumann (the girl in the dark dress with the white collar). Roeckell, like his father and uncle before him, later worked for Steinway & Sons.

This page from Steinway & Sons' 1888 catalog shows the company's New York holdings, which included the "piano case and action factory" in Astoria and the "finishing manufactory" in Manhattan. Interestingly, this catalog also marked the last time the square grand was advertised by Steinway, as the company had by then focused its efforts on the elegant grands in high demand by wealthy Americans.

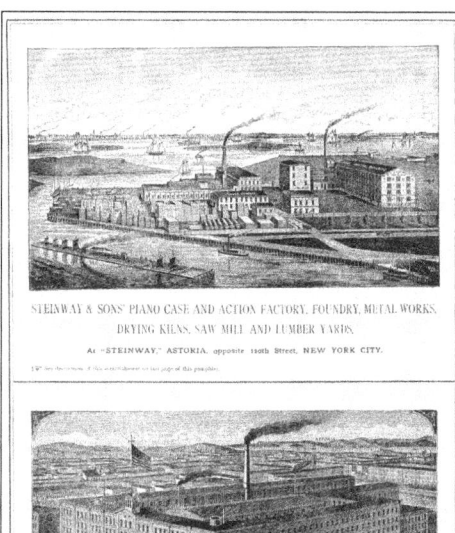

Steinway Village was populated mostly by German-born tradesmen and their families, largely because William Steinway was a savvy marketer. This advertising circular, written in German, offers house lots for sale in Steinway Village in Astoria in 1880. "House Building Plots," it proclaims. Messaging promises "valuable real estate at an affordable opportunity for manufacturers."

Häuser und Bauplätze

— auf —

STEINWAY & SONS'

werthvollem Grundbesitz zu "Steinway", Long Island City,

am East River, gegenüber der 110.—120. Str. New York's.

400 Acker vorzüglichen Landes, nivellirt und in Bauplätze eingetheilt, mit breiten Avenues und Strassen, entsprechend dem allgemeinen Plane Long Island City's.

Eine günstige Gelegenheit für Fabrikanten

und Solche, die den Wunsch hegen, bequeme und freundliche Heimstätten mit Stadtcomfort zu bewohnen.

Entfernungen.

2½ Meilen vom Central-Park, N. Y.; 6 Meilen von City Hall, N. Y.; 1¾ Meilen von 92. Str.-Ferry. Die Wagen der Steinway und Hunter's Point-Pferdebahn laufen direkt durch das Besitzthum in 15 Minuten zur 92. Str.-Ferry; ebenfalls durch Ravenswood und das deutsche Settlement nach der Hunter's Point-Ferry, nach 34. Str. und James' Slip, N. Y.

Die Lage des ganzen Platzes ist hoch

und gesund; schöne Fernsicht über den East River und New York.

Ueber 700 substantielle Villen etc.

sind bereits errichtet und von einer durchaus höchst respektablen Klasse Leute bewohnt.

Gelegenheit in Fülle

für bequemen Schiffsverkehr. 4000 Fuss Wasserfront, wovon bereits 1100 Fuss mit "Bulkheads" und "Docks" vorhanden sind. Gutes Trinkwasser. Die Long Island City-Wasserwerke sind mit jedem Hause in Steinway verbunden. Vorzügliches Abzugs-System. Gas, telephonische und Postverbindung.

Liberale Arrangements

werden mit Fabrikanten und allen andern respektablen Personen getroffen, welche Bauplätze oder fertige Häuser kaufen wollen, und zum Bau Darlehen auf Hypothek gemacht. Wegen weiterer Information wende man sich gefälligst an

STEINWAY & SONS, East 14th Street, New York,
oder STEINWAY LAND OFFICE, 931 Steinway Ave., Steinway, L. I. City.

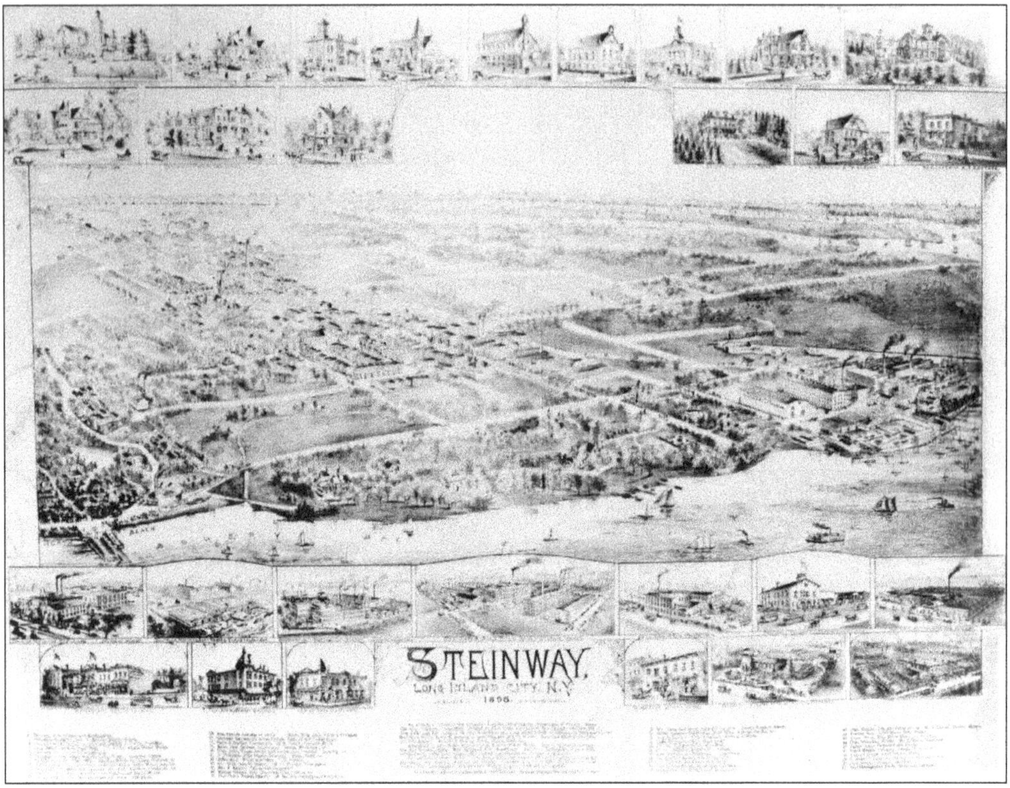

This lithograph depicts Steinway Village in 1896, the year of William Steinway's death. The visionary's dream of a self-contained company town had been realized; however, his goal of removing his piano workers from the influence of organized labor would never entirely come to fruition. Organized labor would simply follow the workers to Astoria.

Three men stand in front of the Astoria Ninety-Second Street trolley in this undated photograph. Steinway houses are visible in the background. Thanks to Steinway's Rikers power plant, Astoria became one of the first areas in the country to use electric trolley cars. The trolley lines connected railroads to ferry stations.

This 1908 photograph depicts the administrative offices of the Steinway factory at Rikers. The first Steinway factory site in Queens was located on Riker Avenue, near Bowery Bay and across from what is now La Guardia Airport. "We sought a place outside the city," William Steinway wrote in his diary, "to escape the machinations of the anarchists and socialists . . . [who] were continually breeding discontent among our workmen, and inciting them to strike." The new factory, built in 1873, housed an iron foundry and a huge lumberyard capable of storing five million square feet of wood. However, the Rikers location suffered problems with moisture, and the heavy humidity near the bay proved a thorny issue to contend with for a manufacturing business steeped heavily in rot-prone wood. In 1901, in his fifth year as president of the company, William's nephew Charles H. Steinway built a second location about a mile away on Ditmars Avenue.

Steinway & Sons was not the first enterprise to develop a company town as a means of corralling its workforce into a controlled setting. Hershey, Pennsylvania, and Pullman, Illinois, (named for a chocolate empire and a railroad sleeping car innovator, respectively) also created company towns around the same time that Steinway Village was growing in Astoria. William Steinway's strategy was straightforward. Between 1870 and 1871, he purchased more than 400 acres of wooded waterfront and meadowlands in northwest Queens. On part of this parcel, he built a new factory, and around the factory, he began construction of houses for his workers, making the new residences available for rent or purchase. The houses in the photograph below are possibly on Twentieth Avenue, just east of Steinway Street on the north side. All real estate transactions, service, and rent collection on these company homes were conducted by Steinway & Sons.

This is a backyard view of the Steinway & Sons factory at Ditmars around 1915. At this site, workers received parts from Rikers, finished cases, regulated keys and actions, and completed final assembly of Steinway pianos before they were shipped out to Steinway Hall and other showrooms around the country and to the new Steinway Hall in London.

In the early 1900s, Queens adopted a street numbering practice based on Philadelphia's grid, in which lower-numbered streets begin near the water and increase further inland. Here, girls pose in front of Astoria's Public School No. 8 on Steinway Street between Ditmars Boulevard and Twenty-third Avenue. These are most likely children of Steinway factory workers. Pictured are, from left to right, Charlotte Schmidt Moeller, Madeline Moeller, Charlotte Moeller, and Maryann Moeller.

This portrait of Steinway & Sons office workers was taken in 1918 at the factory on Ditmars Avenue. Note the World War I posters on the wall behind the group. Despite losses in Hamburg and at the London showroom, Steinway & Sons prospered in the United States during the war. In fact, the year 1916 marked a record-breaking milestone for piano production—6,561 pianos were built in New York, the most in Steinway history.

This photograph was taken during World War II, sometime between 1942 and 1944. It shows the Steinway & Sons Rikers factory with a black outline drawn around the perimeter. North of the line is the abandoned Oaks Logwood Dye Factory. Across the creek is the Con Edison coal pile.

This is the east group of Rikers factory buildings in 1885. Two men and a policeman can be seen in the foreground. This was the year the famous Flood Rock explosion was undertaken by the US Army Corps of Engineers, which opened up the previously treacherous "Hell Gate" passage in the East River. Fifty thousand spectators lined the shores of the East River to watch the explosion.

This composite view shows the Steinway & Sons factories and lumber storage in Astoria around 1920. Steinway's second president, Charles H. Steinway, died of the flu in 1919, leaving his brother Frederick to take the reins. Fred Steinway was to shepherd the company through the Roaring Twenties and would add a new two-story, million-dollar addition to the Ditmars factory. At this time, business was booming—in 1925, Steinway & Sons' piano sales totaled nearly $8 million.

By most accounts, Charles H. Steinway was a shrewd businessman. Grandson of founder Henry E. and second son of Charles G., "Charlie" stepped into Steinway leadership after the death of his uncle William, who had steered the Steinway ship for more than three decades and who had made the name Steinway a household word. Charlie wisely kept two Steinway men as his close counsel. As head of the factory, he relied upon his brother Frederick (later to become the company's third president), and to pioneer piano engineering, he relied upon his cousin Henry Ziegler. This triumvirate was to prove incredibly effective. During Charlie's presidency, Steinway & Sons posted record profits, introduced new piano models, enjoyed robust sales in Europe, and successfully weathered the storms of World War I. This portrait of Charlie was taken in 1916.

This group of children and women stands on a hill (now gone) on Theodore Street. Several streets in Astoria were once named after members of the Steinway family. Theodore Street is current-day Forty-First Street. Nearby Albert Street is current-day Forty-Second Street. Pictured are, from left to right, (first row) Rose Hauschuld, two unidentified children, and Margaret Hauschuld; (second row) four unidentified children; (third row) Adelaide Miller, Willie Brandelick III, and two unidentified children; (fourth row) Mrs. Brandelick, Mrs. Miller, and two unidentified children.

The *Steinway* ferry, pictured here around 1900, transported pianos and workers between Manhattan and Astoria. William Steinway was heavily involved in mass transit in New York City. He was the first commissioner of rapid transit and headed a commission exploring the idea of an underground mass transit system that sowed the seeds for later development of the New York subway system.

Ferryboat "Steinway" of the 92nd Street–Astoria ferry

This is the ferryboat *Steinway* of the Ninety-Second Street–Astoria ferry system. In addition to William's personal interest in transportation systems, Steinway & Sons had a vested interest in facilitating easy travel between Astoria and Manhattan, given that it had men, machinery, and pianos on both sides of the East River.

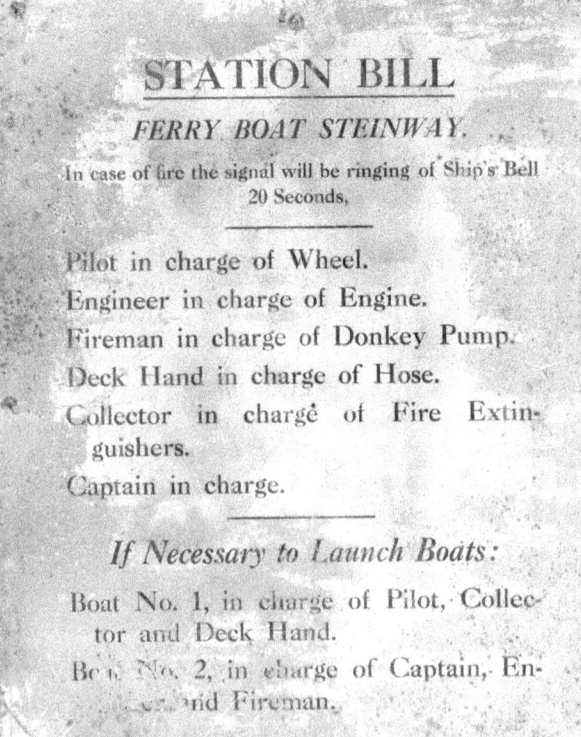

STATION BILL

FERRY BOAT STEINWAY.

In case of fire the signal will be ringing of Ship's Bell 20 Seconds.

Pilot in charge of Wheel.
Engineer in charge of Engine.
Fireman in charge of Donkey Pump.
Deck Hand in charge of Hose.
Collector in charge of Fire Extinguishers.
Captain in charge.

If Necessary to Launch Boats:

Boat No. 1, in charge of Pilot, Collector and Deck Hand.
Boat No. 2, in charge of Captain, Engineer and Fireman.

Rhinebeck & Kingston Ferry Co.

An undated station bill provides direction for emergency procedures in the event of fire or other disaster. The potential for danger was real. The early 20th century saw a number of vessel disasters, including the 1904 fire and sinking of the *General Slocum* steamboat in the East River. The tragedy, which claimed the lives of more than 1,000 people, would surely have been on the minds of Steinway ferry operators.

Material handling: Theodore Cassebeer, Long Island fac-

Wearing a felt hat, Theodore Cassebeer, great-grandson of Henry E. Steinway, is pictured here in the factory lumberyard at Rikers in 1925. Cassebeer served as factory manager under the presidencies of his two cousins, Charlie and Frederick. He was a talented innovator and developed unique improvements to piano rim manufacturing and veneering.

These children of Steinway workers brave a chilly day in 1916. They lived in different apartments in the same Steinway-owned house. Although the company village construct enabled Steinway to wield a great deal of control over its workforce, most Steinway workers living in Steinway houses accepted the benefits of company housing along with the restrictions.

This group of German workers in Astoria is made up mostly of employees of Steinway & Sons. Residents of Steinway's company housing, like these men, were constrained by William Steinway's rules. By controlling housing, transportation, and community services in Steinway Village, Steinway & Sons could keep the pressure on its workforce and discourage any movement toward organized labor or—one of William's biggest fears—strikes.

These Steinway office workers are pictured in 1921 at the Rikers factory. Joe Pirola is at the rear desk in glasses, and Ralph Siedersleben is the bookkeeper in the front. The man with the coat is Frank Cronin, and next to him is Harold Dawber, who was assistant superintendent. At the switchboard is Rose E. Waleri, one of the first women to be employed at Steinway & Sons.

Three important Steinway "bosses," all extended cousins of the Steinway family, confer on a park bench in Astoria in 1932. Pictured from left to right are Paul Bilhuber, Theodore Cassebeer, and Frederick Vietor. This was during a period of abysmal sales and terrible financial straits for Steinway & Sons; in fact, the factory was officially closed from 1931 to 1933.

After limping along through two years of closures and part-time production, the factory reopened at the end of 1933—but 1934 was subsequently the worst year for piano sales in Steinway's history. Fortunately, by 1935, when this photograph of tuner Joseph E. Timms was taken, the market had started to slowly recover.

The site that is today covered with the runways and terminals of La Guardia Airport was once the location of North Beach Amusement Park, opened by William Steinway in 1886. North Beach was wildly popular, attended by up to 50,000 people on a weekend day in summer. The carnival park featured music, drinking, dancing, fishing, weekly fireworks displays, and swan boat or gondola rides in Bowery Bay. Powered by the Steinway power plant, the theme park dazzled New Yorkers, many of whom had never seen electric lights before. Park rides included a roller coaster, Ferris wheel, and carousel. Above it all hung a huge sign that read, "Welcome—W. Steinway & Sons." This family poses for a photograph in an automobile at North Beach Amusement Park in 1925. Pictured from left to right are Louis Berger and his sons Henry and Louis Jr. The father was foreman of Steinway's yard gang.

Six

STEINWAY HALL
CENTER OF MUSIC AND CULTURE

A quarter of the way into the new century, Steinway & Sons opened a new concert hall and showroom on Fifty-Seventh Street in Manhattan. This new Steinway Hall, just a stone's throw from Carnegie Hall, was to become a "piano mecca" in a bigger and more prominent way than its predecessor on Fourteenth Street. Built in 1925, the second Steinway Hall saw the most famous piano artists of all time walk through its doors—many to play in the upstairs concert hall and many more to select performance instruments from the famous piano bank in the basement. In Steinway Hall, Vladimir Horowitz and Sergei Rachmaninoff famously met and practiced together, and the hall saw regular visits from the likes of Arthur Rubinstein, Van Cliburn, Judy Collins, Lang Lang, Billy Joel, Evgeny Kissin, Diana Krall, and Harry Connick Jr. Countless performances took place in both the glamorous upstairs recital hall and the glittering domed reception room. Generations of Steinway men and women celebrated the good years and cursed the bad—often with a stiff drink to accompany both—in the offices of the upper floors. The headquarters of the New York Philharmonic, which was housed in Steinway Hall for many years, was once burglarized here, and in a dark turn, Steinway Hall showcased Steinway-manufactured coffins during World War II. For nearly nine decades, Steinway Hall at Fifty-Seventh Street was the grand piano dame of Midtown. In 2016, Steinway Hall embarked on a new legacy in a new location, where Steinway's legendary instruments continue to make their mark on musical history.

This photograph of Steinway Hall at 109 West Fifty-Seventh Street was taken a few years after its completion. By the turn of the century, Steinway & Sons was producing more than 3,000 pianos a year. The company closed Steinway Hall on Fourteenth Street in favor of a new showroom located in an upscale retail district on Fifty-Seventh Street, close to venerable Carnegie Hall. As early as 1916, Steinway & Sons was under contract to purchase five residential houses on Fifty-Seventh and Fifty-Eighth Streets in preparation for the build. But when New York City adopted innovative new zoning laws, the Steinways were left in a pickle; their planned piano showroom exceeded the new zoning laws' height restrictions. An attempt to rescind agreements to purchase the houses on Fifty-Seventh and Fifty-Eighth Streets resulted in a protracted legal dispute, which spanned years and brought the future of the new hall into question.

Finally, after Steinway was ordered to honor its commitments to the real estate purchases, and eight years after drafting the initial plan, Steinway & Sons' board of trustees voted to move forward with the construction of its opulent new showroom at 109 West Fifty-Seventh Street.

Frederick T. Steinway, Charles G. Steinway's third son, was the third president of Steinway & Sons. He assumed the helm upon the death of his brother Charlie in 1919. It was under Frederick's watch that the new Steinway Hall was set up to become the piano mecca for artists, music lovers, and deep-pocketed piano buyers. Frederick T. Steinway would die of a heart attack just two years after Steinway Hall's opening gala.

Architects Warren and Wetmore had a $3-million budget, and they went all the way with their design for Steinway Hall. The building rises 12 stories and then is set back with a four-story tower and capped with a hipped-roof penthouse. While nowhere near as lavish as the original performance spaces inside Steinway Hall on Fourteenth Street, the new concert hall was on the third floor and presented its own charms.

Steinway & Sons rented out the upper floors in Steinway Hall, including suites to both the New York Philharmonic and its rival the Symphony Society of New York. Studio 1 of radio station WABC was located in the penthouse. This image shows the Skylight Room, a piano showroom. Steinway Hall opened in the same year that saw the publication of *The Great Gatsby* and the launch of the *New Yorker*.

Steinway Hall's window, at the base of the handsome Neoclassical structure, was framed by Ionic columns and capped by a lunette featuring a sculpture of Apollo accepting his muse's crown of musical triumph. The window arced deeply into the interior with a single piece of curved glass. The result was a shadowbox effect that gave the impression that there was no glass at all.

For nearly nine decades, Steinway Hall at Fifty-Seventh Street was the grand dame of Midtown's piano mecca. This photograph depicts administrative offices.

Despite the festivity surrounding its birth, Steinway Hall weathered tough times in its infancy. Two years before the market crash of 1929, Fred Steinway, a visionary businessman who had ridden high on the boom of the prior decade, died suddenly. The reins of the Steinway presidency were left to Fred's cousin Theodore just as the start of one of the most challenging eras in company history began. These photographs depict the iconic Model D in Steinway Hall's grand rotunda.

Steinway & Sons' upper management is pictured at Steinway Hall shortly after Frederick T. Steinway's death in July 1927. From left to right are (sitting) new president Theodore E. Steinway, Henry Ziegler, and William R. Steinway; (standing) Theodore Cassebeer, Paul Schmidt, Fred Vietor, and Charles F.M. Steinway.

The future of the hall's ownership was coming into question by the mid-20th century. Henry Z. Steinway, the company's fifth president, took the helm in 1955, and he was never convinced that maintaining ownership of "that expensive place," as he called Steinway Hall, made good business sense. In 1958, he oversaw the sale of the building to the Manhattan Life Insurance Company for $3 million. Steinway Hall would remain out of the company's ownership for the next 41 years.

The male Steinways are pictured in 1932, financially one of the worst years in company history. From left to right are (sitting) Paul Schmidt, Theodore Cassebeer, Frederick Steinway, Theodore E. Steinway, William Vietor, and William R. Steinway; (standing) Carl Vietor, Theodore D. Steinway, Charles F.M. Steinway, Henry Z. Steinway, Frederick A. Vietor, Charles F.G. Steinway, and John H. Steinway. An interesting note—Henry Ziegler sat for this photograph, but after his death, a cut-out of Theodore Cassebeer's head was placed atop Ziegler's body. The final composite photograph is included here.

In 1951, Steinway Hall was the site of a celebration for employees who had served Steinway for 50 years. Pictured are, from left to right, (sitting) Joseph E. Timms, Frank Peterson, William R. Steinway, Theodore R. Steinway, Emil Unger, Louis Bieler, and Mathias Neizmann; (standing) Herman Gregory, Arthur Boll, John Bushman, Ernest Misfeldt, Harry Manley, Charles Wolde, Charles Roeckell, and G. Ward.

Steinway Hall had a long relationship with the New York Philharmonic, the oldest symphony orchestra in the United States. The orchestra rented space in the first Steinway Hall on Fourteenth Street from 1866 through 1891 and, later, took up residence in the upper floors of Steinway Hall on Fifty-Seventh Street. In this photograph, taken in March 1942, a cake is cut at Steinway Hall in celebration of the Philharmonic's 100th anniversary. It was a somber year to celebrate a centennial. Three months earlier, American radio listeners heard CBS news correspondent Charles Daly break into Arthur Rubinstein's performance with the Philharmonic in order to announce the attack on Pearl Harbor. Cutting the cake is music director John Barbirolli; looking on are, from left to right, Michael Piastro, Mrs. Barbirolli, Ruth Steinway, Mrs. Piastro, Arthur Judson, Meta Von Bernuth, and Manhattan congresswoman Ruth Pratt.

In 1954, William R. Steinway stands with Jack C. Deagan of J.C. Deagan, Inc., a manufacturer of chimes and percussion instruments. These large chimes were installed atop Steinway Hall on Fifty-Seventh Street. Deagan's bells and chimes were placed in several famous installations across the United States, including the 97-bell carillon at Stephen Foster Folk Culture Center State Park in Florida, which is one of the largest musical instruments ever produced.

Steinway Hall was the headquarters for a new era of artist development. Ernest Urchs headed up the Concert & Artist Department and cultivated the careers of Ignacy Paderewski and a young Vladimir Horowitz. This trend toward artist support would come to define Steinway for the next century. Urchs died of a heart attack while on the job at Steinway Hall. He was succeeded by Alexander Greiner (left), pictured here with William R. Steinway (right) and an unidentified woman (center) in 1955.

Vladimir Horowitz was a favorite of the House of Steinway since his debut in Berlin in 1926, when he was courted by Steinway staff in Germany for his endorsement. In an expensive Steinway advertising campaign launched in 1927, an image of Horowitz was paired with the company's first use of the slogan "The Instrument of the Immortals." Horowitz was devoted to Steinway and unerringly loyal to the brand. He was carefully attended to by Steinway & Sons, first by Concert & Artist Department manager Ernest Urchs and, later, by his successor Alexander Greiner. It was in the basement of Steinway Hall that Vladimir Horowitz and Sergei Rachmaninoff had their infamous meeting where they played Rachmaninoff's Third Piano Concerto. Horowitz is pictured here in 1955 at Steinway Hall with Oscar Levant (seated with Horowitz), Alexander Greiner (bow tie), and John H. Steinway. "I am happy that the Steinway has been my faithful and inseparable friend since the inception of my concert career," Horowitz would later write.

Dame Myra Hess (center) was a Steinway Artist and an important presence at Steinway Hall. A personal friend of Julia Steinway, Frederick Steinway's wife, Hess is pictured here in 1958 at a reception at Steinway Hall with Polly Steinway and her husband, Henry Z. Steinway.

The Steinway family maintained a tradition of focusing on the lineage of the male descendants of founder Henry E. Steinway. In this photograph, taken in 1959, several generations of male descendants are commemorated in front of portraits of Henry E. and Julianne at Steinway Hall. Pictured are, from left to right, (sitting) Theodore A., Theodore D., Robert C., Christian T., Henry E., and William R.; (standing) John H., Frederick, Frederick E., Henry Z., Daniel K., William T., and Charles F.G.

The "secrets" of tuning the pianos of the world's great artists go out on the air as William Hupfer (left), chief concert technician of Steinway & Sons, demonstrates to Jo Sherman of NBC's *Monitor* weekend radio program and Frederick Steinway at Steinway Hall Fifty-Seventh Street in 1960. *Monitor* ran for 20 years, from 1955 to 1975.

In 1964, Steinway Artist Leon Fleischer (left) examines exhibits at Steinway Hall with Henry Z. Steinway. The display features memorabilia from Fleischer's career and marks his 20th anniversary before the concert-going public. "The ineffable beauty and sensitivity of a Steinway provide the ideal basis for the realization of great music," wrote Fleischer in his Steinway endorsement.

At a 1964 Steinway Hall reception honoring the 10th anniversary of Van Cliburn's New York debut, Cliburn (center) and his host Henry Z. Steinway (right) greet impresario Sol Hurok (left) in the photograph above. In the photograph below, at the same reception, Van Cliburn gathers with Ruth Steinway (far left); his parents, Rildia and Harvey Cliburn; and Polly and Henry Z. Steinway (far right). Cliburn was a Steinway Artist and a devoted friend to the company. Six years prior to this photograph, the young Texan made global history when, playing a Steinway Model D, he won first prize in the Soviet Union's International Tchaikovsky Piano Competition.

In 1965, Alfred Lotto (left) and Sascha Goradmitzki (right), cowinners in the Montreal International Piano Competition, sit with Henry Z. Steinway (center) in the famed Steinway Hall basement piano bank. The basement housed more than 100 concert grands that were available for Steinway Artists to use for concerts, often at nearby Carnegie Hall or other famous venues.

Steinway & Sons has always seen the value in partnering with music teachers and in supporting piano education. In 1966, Steinway welcomed the Music Education League to Steinway Hall for a program. League president Audray Roslyn Stone, at far left, spoke on "The Parent's Role in Successful Music Study for the Average Child." Eighteen student league members performed at the hall, and the program was introduced by John H. Steinway (standing at rear).

In times of labor unrest, Steinway Hall provided a more visible site for protest than the remote factory in Queens. Members of Local No. 102, American Federation of Labor and Congress of Industrial Organizations (AFL-CIO), picket in front of Steinway Hall in 1970 during a seven-week strike that ultimately proved disappointing for the union, netting the workers little more than the standard yearly pay raise.

Steinway & Sons maintains a tradition of celebrating historic milestones. Here, John H. Steinway, brother of fifth president Henry Z. Steinway, addresses a gathering at the 60th anniversary celebration of Steinway Hall. By all accounts, John loved the spotlight. He was an amateur actor and served for a time as Steinway's head of advertising and public relations.

Here, Steinway Artist Marcus Roberts (left) plays a grand in Steinway Hall. With him are, from left to right, Gene Inman, Kay Blackhurn, and Peter Goodrich. Goodrich worked with Steinway for 35 years and served as head of the Concert & Artist Department. The painting behind the group is just one piece in a vast collection once housed in Steinway Hall, including magnificent, one-of-a-kind instruments from Steinway's custom-made Art Case collection and specially designed pianos from the Limited Edition series. When the building was constructed in 1925, the Steinway family commissioned original paintings that would evoke a rich visual landscape throughout Steinway Hall. Original oil paintings depict composers, such as Berlioz, Chopin, Handel, Mozart, and Wagner, or legendary pianists, such as Franz Liszt, Ignacy Paderewski, Sergei Rachmaninoff, and Anton Rubinstein. Many distinguished artists were represented, including Rockwell Kent, N.C. Wyeth, and Charles Chambers.

Steinway Hall also functioned as a museum honoring the evolution of music since Steinway's founding in 1853. Just behind the rotunda, a gallery housed memorabilia collected by five generations of Steinways. Included in the display cases were awards and medals, insignias noting the firm's appointment as official supplier of pianos to the world's most famous concert halls, scale models of historic Steinway pianos, and displays of meticulously crafted parts used in Steinway pianos.

In 1949, Theodore Steinway sent out a Christmas card with a stately photograph of Steinway Hall embossed on the front. "May the new year bring to us all the things we strive for," he wrote, "a better understanding among men, a happier world and a vision of fine and great things to come." In 2001, Steinway Hall was declared a New York City landmark. The hall is pictured here shortly before its closure in 2014. A new Steinway Hall was built at 1133 Avenue of the Americas.

Seven

A Time of Transition
Steinway during the War

In the February 22, 1944 (Washington's birthday), edition of the company newsletter *Steinway News*, company president Theodore E. Steinway wrote a poignant missive to his four sons and all the Steinway employees serving in the military. "On this day, and every day, we honor and celebrate the name of all the 'Steinway' boys in the service of our country! May they come back to us soon! The House of Steinway needs them and wants them." Theodore was understandably pensive. The year prior, Steinway's administrative headquarters in Germany had been burned to the ground, and not long after, the Hamburg factory was bombed. A decade after struggling through the Great Depression, Steinway & Sons was forced to scramble for new products to manufacture in order to stay in business, given the war rationing on materials crucial to piano-making. It was a difficult time for Steinway & Sons and for its president in particular. But by 1953, as Steinway celebrated its centennial anniversary, seeds of change and recovery were being planted. In 1955, Theodore was succeeded in the Steinway presidency by his son Henry Z. Steinway, a driven businessman with an eye toward profit. The difficult war years were a fading memory when, in 1958, the young Texan Van Cliburn became an international phenomenon by winning the International Tchaikovsky Piano Competition in Moscow seated at a Steinway grand piano.

Theodore E. Steinway served as the company's president from the time of his brother Frederick's death in 1927 until his own retirement in 1955. The son of the venerable William Steinway, Theodore was part of a powerful lineage, and expectations for his leadership were high. Unfortunately, he took the reins of the company when it was on the precipice of financial collapse, and he had the unenviable job of leading Steinway through the Depression years and the uncertainties of World War II. When he resigned suddenly in 1955, all eyes turned to his son Henry Z. Steinway, then only 40 years old, as the only suitable candidate for the presidency of the world's most renowned piano manufacturer.

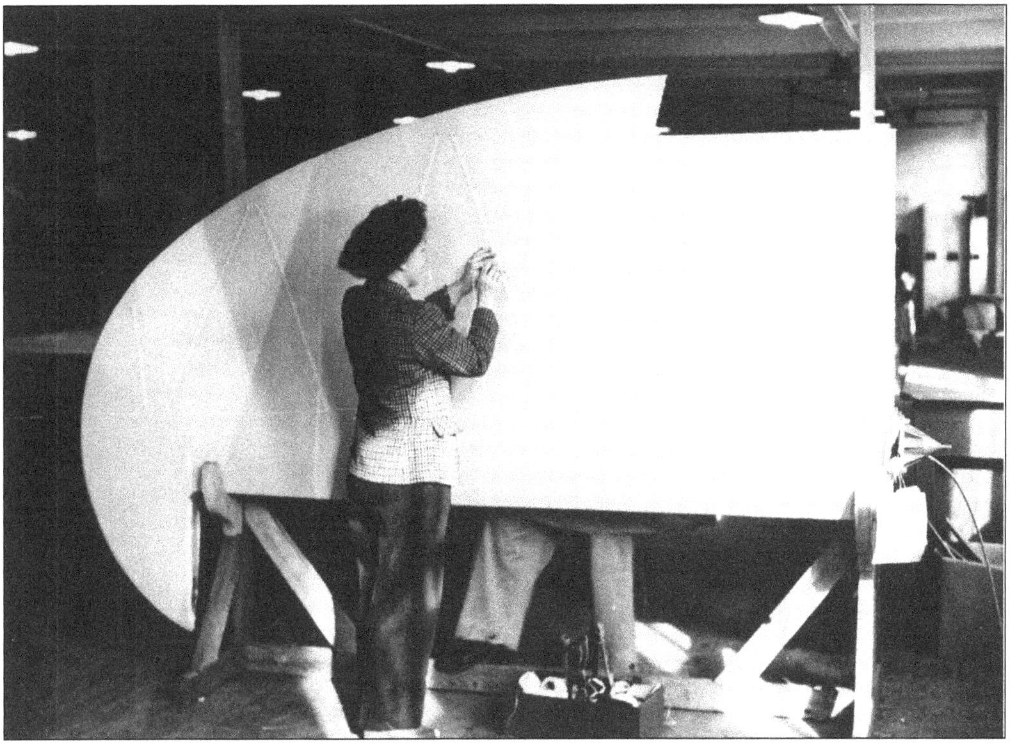

World War II presented peculiar challenges to Steinway & Sons. With a factory in Hamburg, the company was forced to deal with a sense of divisiveness on both sides of the Atlantic—there was hostility against Steinway's German heritage in America and hostility against Steinway's American business in Germany. In addition, building materials for pianos were suddenly unavailable due to war rationing of copper, iron, brass, and felt. Steinway & Sons had to think creatively in order to keep the factory open during the war. Theodore entered into three subcontracts with General Aircraft between 1942 and 1944 to build wooden gliders that would convey troops behind enemy lines. Pictured above, a woman is covering the rudder of a Waco CG-4A glider at the Steinway factory. Below is a similar glider under tow.

Upon entering into glider production, Steinway & Sons was forced to reckon with the challenge of retraining piano-makers—many of whom were highly skilled but either illiterate or non-English-speaking—to learn how to build aircraft. A talented plant manager named Frank Walsh took on the job and helped the hundreds of workers employed at the Astoria factory devise ways of learning and implementing new ways to use their manufacturing skills. In the photograph above, a man works on a glider wing in 1943; he is removing nailing strips after they have been glued to the wing nose. In the photograph below, a man hitches a tow rope to a CG-4A glider.

The glider work of World War II presented an opportunity for women to work at Steinway & Sons in numbers unseen since the company's founding in 1853. These women are brushing dope on glider wings in 1943. Most women working at Steinway & Sons during the war were let go upon the return of the men whose jobs they filled.

Building 1,100 gliders kept Steinway & Sons in business during the war, but there was no great profit to be gained. The finished product was mostly effective at deploying troops, as pictured above, but ineffective as a business venture for Steinway. In 1944, the company lost more than $500,000.

On January 14, 1943, a group of Special Service Unit soldiers at Fort Meade, Maryland, gather around a Steinway & Sons "Victory Vertical" upright piano. The Victory Vertical model was the brainchild of three Steinway administrators (Roman de Majewski, Edward Orcutt, and Sascha Greiner) as a way to get the company out of aircraft production and back into piano production.

ano, 1943

Steinway built nearly 2,436 Victory Verticals, also called the "G.I. Piano." It was a small piano that four men could lift. It came in olive drab, gray, or blue and was designed to be carried aboard ships or dropped by parachute from an airplane to bring music to the soldiers. Steinway & Sons saw 228 workers serve in World War II; all but five came back. (Courtesy US Army Signal Corps.)

The Victory Vertical was mostly a standard Steinway upright, with several modifications. It was 40 inches high and weighed 500 pounds. With no legs, the piano sat sturdily on the floor. It was transported in an olive-drab packing crate with handles for easy carrying. (Courtesy San Diego Air & Space Museum.)

In this photograph, which was published in Steinway's company newsletter in October 1944, Pvt. William Kuehl tunes a Victory Vertical in the music repair shop on Guadalcanal. (Courtesy San Diego Air & Space Museum.)

The tropical climates of many theaters of war would have wreaked havoc on ivory keys. Instead, the Victory Vertical models were fitted with celluloid keys and had soft iron (instead of rationed copper) wrapped around the steel bass strings. Seated at a Victory Vertical is baritone Benjamin DeLoache (foreground), who taught for many years at the Yale School of Music. (Courtesy San Diego Air & Space Museum.)

Here, soldiers strike up the band, including a Steinway Victory Vertical, in the Philippines. In 1943, a private named Kenneth Kranes wrote the following home to his family: "We all got a kick out of it and sure had fun after meals when we gathered around the piana to sing. I slept smiling and even today am humming a few of the songs we sang." Kranes was killed in battle a week later. (Courtesy San Diego Air & Space Museum.)

Rows of Victory Verticals stand at attention at the Steinway & Sons factory in Queens awaiting delivery to the US Army in July 1944. A total of 2,436 Victory Verticals were produced and shipped to the US War Department for the armed forces.

Legendary pianist and longtime friend of the House of Steinway Josef Hofmann plays a Victory Vertical while, from left to right, William R. Steinway and Theodore E. Steinway look on. Theodore endured terrible personal strain during the war years. Steinway & Sons was under tremendous financial pressure, and his four sons were all enlisted—three of them deployed overseas.

Theodore D. Steinway (1914–1982) was the oldest son of Steinway's fourth president, Theodore E. Steinway. He served in the Signal Corps in the South Pacific.

Theodore's second son, Henry Z. Steinway (1915–2008), was tapped for the Steinway & Sons presidency in 1955, when he was only 40 years old, and he would remain in that position until 1977. During the war, he worked on Governor's Island in New York as an Army counterintelligence investigator.

John (1917–1989), the third son of Theodore and Ruth Steinway, served in the Army Air Transport Command. He later served as the company's head of advertising and coordinated a number of performances for presidential state dinners at the White House. Affable, charming, and outgoing, he was a loyal ambassador for the Steinway brand.

Youngest son Frederick "Fritz" Steinway (1921–2004) served in Japan during World War II as a Navy lieutenant. He later went to Harvard Business School and, in 1958, would take over the position of head of Steinway & Sons' Concert & Artist Department after the death of Alexander Greiner.

Myra Hess, a Steinway Artist, instituted a series of lunchtime concerts in England during World War II to compensate for the blackouts of concert halls during evening hours. "For me, the Steinway piano alone can create the illusion of singing," Hess once said.

More than seven million people turned out for a ticker-tape parade in 1951 honoring Gen. Douglas A. MacArthur's service during the Korean War. Steinway Hall on Fifty-Seventh Street was decked out in bunting for the occasion. MacArthur's car is escorted by a police motorcade.

"The Steinway with its beauty and power is the perfect medium for expressing the performer's art—drama and poetry," said Van Cliburn. These photographs depict the incredible phenomenon of the 23-year-old Texan and his Steinway capturing first prize in the 1958 International Tchaikovsky Piano Competition in Moscow. His victory stunned the world and helped diffuse American-Soviet Cold War tensions. Upon his return from Russia, Cliburn was greeted in New York City with a ticker-tape parade, an honor usually reserved for military heroes and heads of state. Since 2000, Van Cliburn's International Piano Competition in Fort Worth, Texas, has been conducted using only Steinway pianos. (Both, courtesy The Cliburn.)

Eight

PEOPLE AND PIANOS
STEINWAY THROUGH THE DECADES

People and Pianos is the title of Theodore E. Steinway's 1953 retrospective of Steinway & Sons, which he wrote in longhand on yellow legal pads on the occasion of the company's 100th birthday. The title is a fitting descriptor of the two forces that have grown to inform cultural associations with the Steinway name, particularly in the 20th century. Steinway is a brand that is intrinsically tied both to the instruments it builds and to the artists who bring those instruments to life. "I know a fine way to treat a Steinway," wrote Irving Berlin in 1915, ushering in an era in which the Steinway piano became a ubiquitous symbol of music, artistry, prestige, and luxury. Today, the Steinway is viewed as the apex of musical artistry as well as the symbol of an American business success story. It is the choice of 98 percent of concertizing artists, and these performers are not paid to endorse the piano. The people presented in the chapter that follows comprise but a tiny sampling of the thousands of performing artists, composers, celebrities, music teachers, students, business leaders, artisans, salespeople, and others who have been swept up in the heart-thundering beauty of the Steinway piano.

The Ranee of Sarawak (Margaret Brooke) plays a Steinway grand around 1910. The cultured and refined Brooke was the wife of the second white rajah of Sarawak, a small country on the coast of Borneo. The couple were both Asian monarchs and English subjects, and the Ranee's memoir, *My Life in Sarawak*, offered a unique glimpse into an exotic culture.

Sergei Rachmaninoff (1873–1943) was one of the most important Steinway Artists of the 20th century and a loyal supporter of Steinway. This illustration of Rachmaninoff was used in Steinway advertising. "Dear Mr. Steinway, I am very happy to have the opportunity of using your pianos for my concerts because I consider them to be perfect in every way," he wrote. "Faithfully yours, Sergei Rachmaninoff."

At the Edward McDowell Benefit Concert in 1927, a who's who of Steinway colleagues and friends is gathered. From left to right are Ernest Urchs, Rhoda Erskine, author and professor John Erskine, music critic Olin Downes, Josef Hofmann, Ernest Hutcheson, George Barrere, George Gershwin, and Richard Singer. Gershwin later wrote a review of the performances of Downes, Urchs, and John Erskine.

Here, from left to right, Princesses Elizabeth and Margaret pose at a Steinway upright inside Buckingham Palace in 1947. Both young women studied piano, and in particular, Margaret was reported to be gifted in music, singing, and acting. Noël Coward wrote the following in his diary: "Princess Margaret surprisingly good. She has an impeccable ear, her piano playing is simple but has perfect rhythm, and her method of singing is really very funny."

Vladimir Horowitz (1903–1989) was arguably the most renowned pianist of the 20th century. His colorful personality and astounding performances enthralled audiences for decades. In 1934, Steinway presented Horowitz and his wife, Wanda, with a Steinway Model D as a wedding present. In the early 1940s, this piano was replaced with a piano known as Concert D No. 503 (CD-503). Steinway & Sons still takes CD-503 on national tours for viewing and playing opportunities.

This ballet performance is part of the "Fashion in Music" program sponsored by Steinway & Sons and Mia Grau. It was held in the grand ballroom of the Waldorf Astoria Hotel in Manhattan on March 6, 1954. The Waldorf Astoria was also the home for many years of Cole Porter's 1907 Steinway grand, which came back to the Steinway factory for restoration in 2019 and will be featured in the newly renovated Waldorf Astoria set to reopen in 2021.

Television personality Ed Sullivan plays the piano as, from left to right, Steinway Artists Beveridge Webster, Moura Lympany, and Eugene List look on. This photograph was taken at a rehearsal for the Steinway Centennial Concert at Carnegie Hall on October 19, 1953. Sullivan aired segments of the rehearsal on his *Toast of the Town* show.

In January of the same year, the Indianapolis Symphony Orchestra delivered a Steinway Centennial Concert at the Murat Theater in Indianapolis. Theodore E. Steinway was determined to put on a brave face for Steinway & Sons throughout its 100th-anniversary year, despite dwindling sales and staggering debt. It would take several years and the new energies of company president Henry Z. Steinway to turn Steinway's financial outlook around.

From left to right, Steinway Artists Constance Keene, Jacques Abram, Muriel Kerr, and Abram Chasins practice on a Steinway at a rehearsal for the Steinway Centennial Concert at Carnegie Hall in New York on October 19, 1953.

This photograph, taken in 1964, depicts the Beaux Arts Trio, comprised of cellist Bernard Greenhouse, violinist Daniel Guillet, and pianist Menahem Pressler at a Steinway piano. The trio had a tremendous performance history, spanning from their debut in 1955 until their farewell performance in 2008. The lineup of other musicians changed throughout the years, but Pressler remained a constant.

The dramatic Italian tenor Mario Del Monaco, nicknamed the "Brass Bull of Milan," is shown at the keyboard of his new white-and-gold hand-carved Louis XV Steinway grand. The photograph is autographed by Del Monaco with the following inscription: "To the best piano of the world with admiration."

Steinway Artist Richard Rodgers (1902–1979) and lyricist Lorenz Hart (1895–1943) are pictured here at a Steinway. In 2004, pianist John Bucchino released a CD titled *On Richard Rodgers' Piano*, featuring Bucchino's interpretations of 16 popular Rodgers compositions performed and recorded on Rodgers's 1939 Steinway grand. The piano was completely restored and is now owned by Rodgers's grandson. (Courtesy Library of Congress, LC-US262-122089.)

Sr. Mariella O.P. of Marycrest High School in Portland, Oregon, plays a Steinway in 1963. The education market—primary, secondary, and college-level—has been an important focus of Steinway & Sons since the early 20th century. Schools that attain the status of "All-Steinway School" commit to using only Steinway pianos in their classrooms, practice rooms, and performance spaces.

Steinway Artist Arthur Rubinstein (1887–1982) was one of the most revered pianists of the 20th century and was a devout loyalist to Steinway. "A Steinway is a Steinway and there is nothing like it in the world," he said. He is pictured here with John Steinway (left) and Henry Z. Steinway (right).

Steinway Artist Roger Williams (right) autographs his record *Solid Gold Steinway* at Macy's in New York City in 1964. In 1955, Williams recorded "Autumn Leaves," the only piano instrumental to reach No. 1 on Billboard's popular music chart. "Only my loyal Steinway endures," Williams wrote. "Be it beaten or caressed, its gorgeous tone remains."

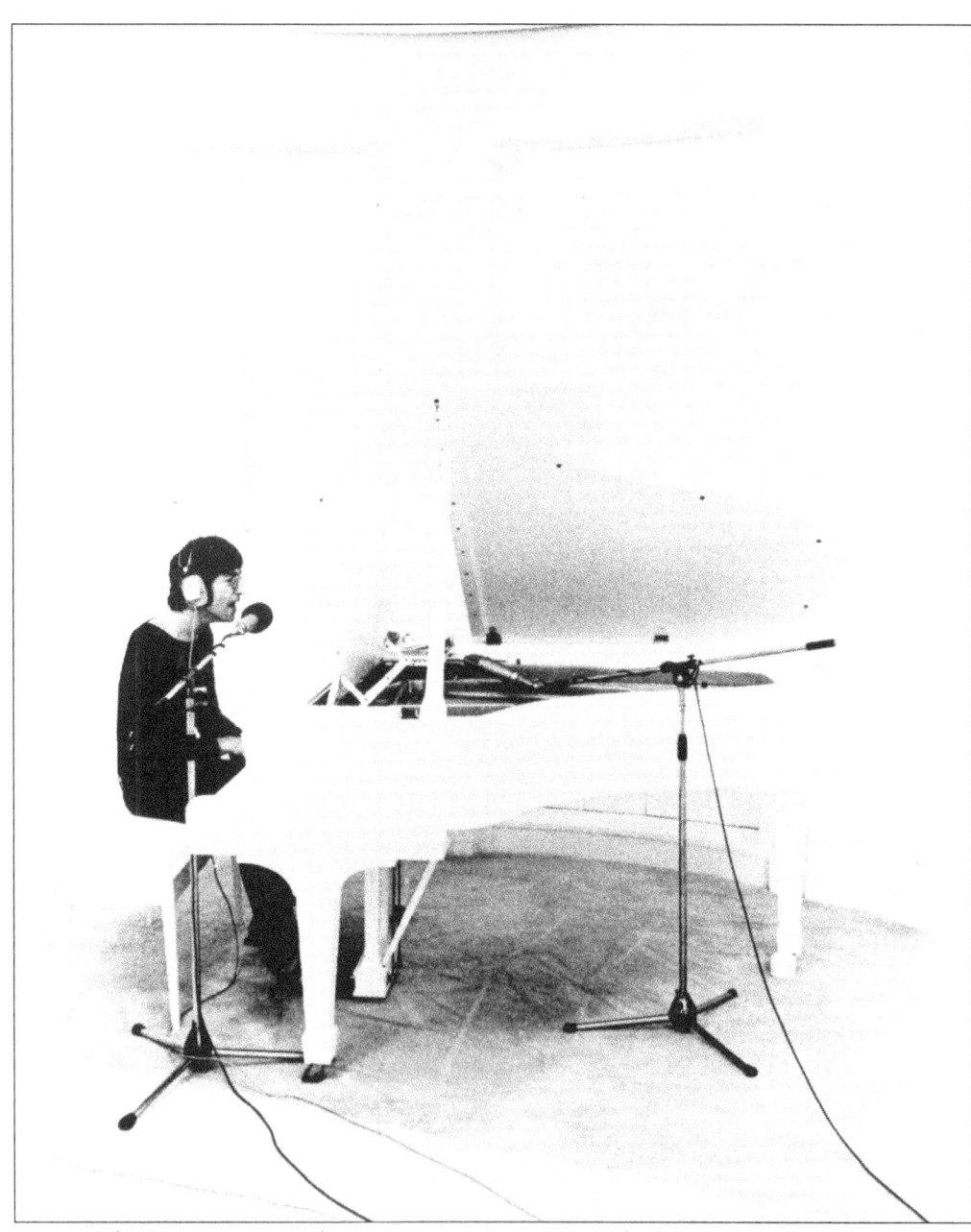

In 1971, John Lennon composed "Imagine" on a Steinway upright that was later sold to the personal collection of the late pop star George Michael. Also in 1971, on her 38th birthday, Lennon gifted his wife, Yoko Ono, with the white Steinway pictured above. In 2010, on what would have been Lennon's 70th birthday, Steinway & Sons introduced a limited-edition piano to commemorate Lennon's contributions to the world of music and his efforts to cultivate world peace. The Imagine Series Limited Edition is modeled after Yoko Ono's birthday piano, which is still at their famous Manhattan apartment in the Dakota Building near Central Park. The lyrics "you may say I'm a dreamer" are displayed on the bass side of the rim on the limited-edition piano, and the opening bars to "Imagine" are printed directly on the piano's plate. A replica of John Lennon's signature is featured on the treble side of the fallboard.

Franz Mohr, pictured above, served as Steinway's chief concert technician for more than a quarter century. He worked closely with luminaries including Vladimir Horowitz, Van Cliburn, Arthur Rubinstein, Rudolf Serkin, Glenn Gould, and others. In his book My Life with the Great Pianists, Mohr wrote, "I play more at Carnegie Hall than anybody else, but I have no audience." Mohr retired from Steinway & Sons in 1992 and was succeeded by Ron Coners, pictured in the photograph below on the far left, standing next to Mohr, middle. Also pictured are Mary Griff of Steinway's Concert & Artist Department and Peter Goodrich, who worked with Steinway for 35 years until his retirement as head of the Concert & Artist Department in 2010. This photograph was taken in Steinway Hall on Fifty-Seventh Street in 1980.

Following Henry Z. Steinway's retirement as Steinway president in 1977 and the sale of Steinway & Sons to CBS in 1972, company leadership was no longer in the hands of a Steinway family member. Pictured above is Steinway's sixth president, Robert P. Bull (far left), looking on as Steinway Artist Ramsey Lewis talks music at Avery Fisher Hall in Manhattan. Also pictured to the right of Bull are, from left to right, Vivian Rubin, Connie Bull, and David W. Rubin, head of Steinway's Concert & Artist Department. Bull served as president for less than two years.

Steinway's seventh president was Peter Perez, who led the company from 1978 to 1982. He is pictured here, far left, in 1981 at a celebration honoring Lionel C. Squibb (holding silver tray along with his wife) for his 50 years of service as Steinway's London branch manager. John H. Steinway is on the far right.

Steinway's eighth president, Lloyd Meyer (left), speaks with guests at a reception for a Carnegie auction at Steinway Hall in 1985. Meyer served as company president from 1982 to 1985, and during his tenure, the company was sold by CBS to brothers John P. and Robert Birmingham.

Steinway leadership since 1985 has been held by, from left to right, Bruce Stevens (from 1985 to 2008), Thomas Kurrer (from 2008 to 2012), and Ron Losby (from 2016 to present). Not pictured is Michael Sweeney (from 2013 to 2016). The Steinway story from the mid-1980s to today has been one of innovation and flexibility to meet the needs of a changing piano market. With the introduction of two new piano lines (the mid-priced Boston and the entry-level Essex), Steinway has expanded its offerings to include both Steinway and Steinway-designed pianos, with the two newer brands manufactured outside the venerable New York factory. In 2016, the company introduced Spirio—the world's finest high-resolution player piano.

Pictured above is Henry Z. Steinway with a limited-edition piano released by Steinway & Sons in 2006 in honor of his 91st birthday. Only 91 such pianos were built, each one with a distinctive music desk featuring the initials HZS in intricate carving. Henry Z.—the last of the Steinway family members to be involved in the day-to-day operations of Steinway & Sons—passed away in 2008. Before his death, he donated his personal collection of Steinway family photographs, administrative files, memorabilia, letters, and more to the La Guardia and Wagner Archives

under the care of Dr. Richard K. Lieberman, a Steinway historian and author of the remarkable book *Steinway & Sons* (1995). Without the donation of Henry Z.'s collection of photographs and records, some of which date back to the 1850s, and without Dr. Lieberman's painstaking research and writing on the topics of the Steinway family and their iconic business, this volume of Images of America would not have been possible.

Visit us at
arcadiapublishing.com

www.ingramcontent.com/pod-product-compliance
Lightning Source LLC
Chambersburg PA
CBHW060938170426
43194CB00027B/2993